JOH

ONE LESS GOD THAN YOU

How to Answer the Slogans,
Clichés, and Fallacies That Atheists
Use to Challenge Your Faith

Catholic
Answers
Press

Published by Catholic Answers, Inc.
2020 Gillespie Way
El Cajon, California 92020
1-888-291-8000 orders
619-387-0042 fax
catholic.com

Printed in the United States of America

Cover and interior by Russell Graphic Design

978-1-68357-165-0
978-1-68357-166-7 Kindle
978-1-68357-167-4 ePub

I'd like to thank Catholic Answers Press for publishing this book. I continue to learn so much about the Faith from people at Catholic Answers. Also, I'd like to thank Gary Michuta for introducing me to CA Press and urging me to publish the book.

Special gratitude goes to my wonderful wife Christine. I thank her for the constant love and support as she encouraged me during many afternoons working on the manuscript. Finally, I'd like to thank Todd Aglialoro and Jeffrey Rubin for their work in the editing process; they shaped this project into a more coherent and useful whole.

CONTENTS

SLOGANS ABOUT FAITH & EVIDENCE

MISCELLANEOUS SLOGANS

INTRODUCTION

You probably think Santa Claus is real. Or that the Earth is flat. Maybe your ancestors thought Thor caused lightning and thunderstorms. Or that praying to a statue would bring healing. We have moved past that. Now, we live in an age of science. If you still believe in God, you must be a superstitious ignoramus.

This common attitude of internet atheists has led many away from faith. Believers must share the blame. A lot of Catholic Christians cannot give reasons for the hope that is within them. They have not learned to support their worldview with reasons and evidence. Rather, they've been told to "just have faith" and not ask too many questions.

Because of this, atheism has been successful in winning converts. Many skeptical slogans have led others to doubt their religious beliefs. But although the slogans have surface-level plausibility, I will show that they do not stand up to scrutiny. Some slogans are more serious than others, and behind several of them are deep, philosophical objections (such as the problem of evil). Nonetheless, all of them can be answered using the intellectual resources from the Christian tradition and contemporary philosophy.

My goal in this book is to equip you with the knowledge and tactics needed to answer the most popular atheist slogans. If you study this material, you will be more than ready to respond the next time you hear skeptical one-liners in conversation.

ATHEISTS ARE GETTING THEM YOUNG

Recently, I was at a retreat where the priest relayed that many elementary students are self-proclaimed atheists by the fourth grade. On the podcast *Every Knee Shall Bow*,[1] the hosts report the rise of atheism among middle and high school students.

One of the hosts, Dave VanVickle, explains that in one case it was a high school science teacher turning students into atheists. Parents came to VanVickle for damage control, asking him to speak with their now-atheist sons and daughters.

In the 1994 anthology *God and the Philosophers*, Michael J. Murray tells what happened during his sophomore year as a philosophy student. Murray's friend had been bothered by a philosophy professor who had been "leaning on" the theists. In fact, that professor admitted to Murray during office hours, "One of my goals is that all of my students leave my class as atheists."[2] This episode occurred in the 1980s.

Almost forty years later, the situation is worse. We need to face the reality of atheism on the rise. Particularly, we need to know how to dialogue about our faith *intelligently*. If we don't, then more of our children will be swept away by the atheist slogans of the age.

FIVE FOUNDATIONAL PRINCIPLES

Interacting with atheists can be draining. Not every conversation will go well, especially when you start out. But if you follow these five principles, you can drastically improve your mindset and your conversations.

Here's the first principle: pray every day. Develop a daily prayer routine. Decide on a specific segment of time as your personal prayer baseline. It could be ten or fifteen minutes. Currently, I aim for twenty minutes, but I don't always hit my mark. But I want to grow in my prayer life. Some spiritual masters recommend thirty minutes per day with the goal of building up to a holy *hour* every day.

The *Catechism of the Catholic Church* sets out the importance of a prayer schedule and routine:

> The choice of the time and duration of the prayer arises from a determined will, revealing the secrets of the heart. One does not undertake contemplative prayer only when one has the time: one makes time for the Lord, with the firm determination not to give up, no matter what trials and dryness one may encounter. One cannot always meditate, but one can always enter into inner prayer, independently of the conditions of health, work, or emotional state. The heart is the place of this quest and encounter, in poverty and in faith (CCC 2710).

This principle drives us to develop a deeper relationship with the Lord. This will allow you to discern more effectively what a person needs to hear in conversation. Also, it will prevent you from getting burned out or discouraged when dialogue goes bad. You don't need me to tell you that conversations about religion often get heated. Daily prayer will help us to keep our cool during such encounters. Even if the other side resorts to insults and mockery, that is not the Christian way. As a result, you will not find mockery in the pages of this book. My aim has nothing to do with making fun of the New Atheists. Rather, I want to equip you to handle skeptics charitably.

As a baptized Christian, you have the indwelling Holy Spirit. Conversing with God every day deepens this reality, allowing the Holy Spirit to work through you. Daily prayer will help you know what to say and how to say it. So that's the first tip: pray every day.

Here's the second principle: whenever possible, start by asking questions rather than making statements. Asking questions places you in the driver's seat of the conversation. You can steer it where you want it to go. You can make sure it stays on topic.

Questions provide an avenue to learn what the other person actually thinks, providing you with valuable information for deciding how to help your conversation partner.

Greg Koukl[3] points to three helpful questions that can be asked in almost any context:

- "What do you mean by that?"
- "How did you come to that conclusion?"
- "Have you ever considered . . . ?"

Questions are powerful. And they're fun! When you dialogue with an atheist, it's much less stressful to ask questions than to try to give a detailed argument from memory.

The more you find out about their beliefs, the better position you are in to help defuse the slogans. **One central aim in this book is to provide you with specific questions you can ask when you hear people raise different slogans.** Also, once you see the power of asking questions, you can start to develop your own questions to use in apologetic/evangelistic contexts.

Here's the third principle: Don't let people get away with vague, wishy-washy criticisms. Sometimes people make vague objections they think are enough to win the day. Consider the following:

- "You know the problem of evil, right? That's why I don't believe in God."
- "You Catholics have that abuse scandal. Who would want to join a corrupt Church like that?"

Too often, we immediately launch into a defense. Before the skeptic elicits a response from us, we must require that he make his criticism clearer, provide more detail, and, whenever possible, give us the fullness of the argument he has in mind.

Consider the first example above. I'd respond, "Tell me more. What do you have in mind concerning the problem of evil? Can you spell it out for me?" These questions encourage the person to clarify, and they also allow you to assess how much homework he has done. Moreover, you don't start floundering around with fancy arguments before understanding what he's saying.

Here's the fourth principle: apologetics is most helpful to those who are *already open* to the truths of faith. I received this tip from Dave VanVickle. An angry, hostile atheist can swiftly resist philosophical argumentation. Even the most powerful arguments may fly right past him as he pulls out his list of grievances against religion.

This principle encourages realistic expectations. The most hardened, angry skeptics need our prayers. Perhaps they've been abused by a priest in the past, or dealt with some other terrible circumstance in life. The Holy Spirit can work on the heart and soften them for future conversations.

On the other hand, those with a sincere desire to understand can be led closer to Christ with answers from the Christian intellectual tradition. But if that's true, should we not even bother with apologetics when talking to those who are closed to faith? Not so fast. VanVickle also argues that apologetics in that circumstance can bolster the faith of the believer making the arguments, or of other believers listening to the conversation. I find this to be exactly right.

I'd summarize VanVickle's points about the use of apologetics in evangelism as follows: 1) arguments and evidence can be helpful to those who are *already open* to the truth about God; 2) they can bolster the faith of believers using the arguments or listening to the conversation; and 3) they're typically ineffective when conversing with atheists who appear to be *closed off* to religion.

Here's the fifth principle: don't neglect the soft skills of evangelism. By "soft skills" I mean the ways of conducting ourselves outside of apologetic encounters. How should we interact with others? I submit that two keys are kindness and treasure recognition. Kindness consists of showing genuine respect for others and developing an interest in understanding their point of view. *Treasure recognition* is a term I developed after a dialogue with Josh Rasmussen.[4]

He pointed out that if in our conversations we fail to treat the other person as a treasure, made in the image of God, then even if our arguments succeed, our manner of proceeding can undermine our goals. As Catholic Christians, we must keep in mind the divinely revealed truth that everyone we encounter is a treasure of intrinsic value whom God commands us to love.[5]

So don't be a jerk. Give more compliments. Be openly Catholic by saying grace before meals, keeping prayers or pictures of saints on your desk, and include Mass in your discussion of the weekends and holidays. These soft skills do not require an advanced apologetic, and they can go a long way toward building trust and plausibility in religion.

J.P. Moreland speaks to the idea of scientism limiting our "plausibility structures"—background assumptions that give rise to a framework for what people find reasonable.[6] A world of religion and miracles seems implausible to those who grew absorbing scientism in their schooling. But when our youth see sober-minded men and women publicly living out their Catholic faith, that can help reshape the plausibility structures they develop.

Not all evangelism requires explicit gospel-preaching. Simply by going about your normal dealings, extending kindness to others, and being openly Catholic, you show Catholicism to be a live, reasonable option.

So that's the fifth principle. Throughout the book, I'll call your attention to these five core principles when it comes to answering atheist slogans.

1. Pray every day.

2. Whenever possible, start by asking questions rather than making statements.

3. Don't let people get away with vague, wishy-washy criticisms.

4. Apologetics is most helpful to those who are *already open* to truths of faith.

5. Don't neglect the soft skills of evangelism.

MY APPROACH TO SLOGANS

First, we'll lay out our structure and method in more detail. Then, in each chapter, I'll present a popular atheist slogan. We'll analyze the objection, and I'll expound on what it means. Some slogans are superficial, but others are more serious and require deep, philosophical engagement.

Next, I'll give you some questions to use in response. These questions move the conversation forward. Also, I'll provide some useful principles and examples that will assist you in the particulars of handling each slogan. Finally, I'll give a short summary of the chapter's content and list resources for further study.

To reiterate: **my goal in this book is to equip you with the knowledge and tactics needed to answer** the most prominent atheist slogans in conversation. How will we pursue that goal?

STRUCTURE AND METHOD

I'm the faculty adviser for our school's chess club. As high school teachers, we get involved with extracurricular activities and interact with students outside of class. Two years ago, my principal asked me to start a chess club. Although I knew how to play, I was not at all acquainted with chess terminology or strategy. For those of you who are, you know how deep and intricate the game is. For those of you who are not, take my word for it that chess is a complex game that you can study for a lifetime!

To help me prepare for advising the club, my brother bought me a book: *The Complete Book of Chess Strategy: Grandmaster Techniques from A to Z* by Jeremy Silman. The book is organized into parts that include the **opening**, the **middlegame**, and the **endgame**.

There's a nice parallel between the game of chess and encounters with atheists and skeptics. An experienced chess player has a big advantage over a player who knows *how* to move the pieces but lacks training in strategy. Although the game might seem balanced at the outset, the experienced player quickly gains advantages over his untrained opponent.

That's sort of how atheists and skeptics can cause big problems for untrained believers. Three or four big opening moves can put you in the driver's seat of a chess game that leads to a brutal checkmate. Three or four slogans can be lobbed at an unassuming Catholic and sow seed that eventually destroys his faith.

In an apologetics encounter, slogans are part of the *opening*. When an atheist hurls one of the twenty slogans our way, our initial response is important. We should clarify the objection and respond with questions. The meat of each chapter will be spent on our opening replies. I strongly suggest that you memorize the important aspects of each opening. If you have some go-to questions to ask, you will be ready to start conversations off on the right foot.

When it comes to asking questions, I distinguish **diagnostic questions** from **dialectical questions**. Diagnostic questions consist of finding out more about how the person conceives of his objection. The aim is to gather information. With dialectical questions, the aim is to expose a weakness or false assumption in your discussion partner's thinking. Recall, in the introduction, I provided the three basic questions expounded on by Greg Koukl in his book *Tactics*:

1. What do you mean by that?
2. How did you come to that conclusion?
3. Have you ever considered . . . ?

These three questions reflect the same order of dialogue described by the 2019 Vatican document *Male and Female He Created Them: Toward a Path of Dialogue on the Question of Gender Theory in Education*. It is worth quoting at some length:

> The methodology in mind is based on three guiding principles seen as best-suited to meet the needs of both individuals and communities: *to listen, to reason, and to propose*. In fact, listening carefully to the needs of the other, combined with an understanding of the true diversity of conditions, can lead to a shared set of rational elements in an argument, and can prepare one for a Christian education rooted in faith that "throws a new light on every-

thing, manifests God's design for man's total vocation, and thus directs the mind to solutions which are fully human" [emphasis mine].[7]

Although the document focuses mainly on issues related to gender, sexuality, and education, the three-step model of **listen-reason-propose** works well for any dialogue. The first questions you ask should foster **listening with an aim of gathering information**; in other words, they should be **diagnostic**. Let's take Koukl's recommendations one by one:

1. WHAT DO YOU MEAN BY THAT?

For example, when someone says, "Science has disproved Christianity," just ask, "What do you mean?" Invite the person to tell you more. Your tone and body language should be welcoming, inquisitive, and exploratory. You want to hear him out! Not for the purpose of burying him, but because he has some issue that you want to get clearer on. You may be able to help him to resolve the issue, or to take a step toward reconsidering it, but if you don't hear him out, or you come off as abrasive and dismissive, this resolution may not be reached. So as the Vatican document says, start by listening.

The document also recommends that we **reason**. In other words, the **listening** phase can lead to "a shared set of rational elements in an argument." Argument gets a bad reputation nowadays. But arguments done well are rational guides to truth. They need not imply quarrelsome encounters. Rather, in the philosophical sense, an argument is a set of steps that lead to a conclusion.[8]

So our next set of questions will be aimed at **reasoning**.

This includes both probing our discussion partner's reasoning and presenting reasons of our own. The go-to question at this step is Koukl's second one:

2. HOW DID YOU COME TO THAT CONCLUSION?

Variants of this question include, "Why do you think that?" or "What are some of your reasons for holding to that position?" We should listen carefully to detect the principles and arguments at play. Also, at this stage we might pose *Socratic* questions intended to draw out further discussion. This often blends with the third stage described by the Vatican document: **to propose.** We can ask questions of the form Koukl recommends:

3. HAVE YOU EVER CONSIDERED . . . ?

By offering something more for the person to contemplate, you require that he update his view or possibly reconsider his position.

Return to the previous example and suppose the conversation went like this:

Friend: Science has disproved Christianity.

You: What do you mean by that?

Friend: Christians think God made all the birds and animals and created the world in six days. But now we know that happened through evolution and millions of years. So science has disproved Christianity.

You: Have you ever considered that some Christians do not deny evolution?[9]

Friend: Yes, but that's because they don't take the Bible literally. But then, it's like what's the point? If the Bible doesn't have to mean what it says, then Jesus and everything can just be a metaphor.

You: So, are you saying Christians must take the entire Bible literally?

Friend: Well, sort of. It's very suspicious that they take the Bible literally until modern science comes along and disproves it. Then they say: actually, no, it's not supposed to be literal!

You: Have you considered that Jews and Christians read some parts of the Bible in a nonliteral fashion well before modern science came on the scene?

Friend: Really? I'm skeptical of that, but what do you have in mind?

You: Well, for example, the Bible is not a single book with a single genre. Rather, it's more like a library with a wide array of books with different genres and subgenres. For example, the Old Testament contains interpretative histories like 1 and 2 Kings. But it also contains proverbs that convey wisdom and advice, as well as poetic psalms and books of religious law or prophecy. The book of Daniel contains apocalyptic visions and symbols. Additionally, some books contain multiple elements, such as Exodus, which consists of the narrative of Moses leading the Jews out of Egypt and the giving of laws to God's people. In the New Testament, we find the Gospels, which are forms of ancient biographies, as well as epistles, or letters, to various churches written by apostles. When it comes to Genesis, some early Christian writers thought the first chapters contained figurative language. St. Augustine famously did not hold to a literal six-day creation story.

Of course, mock conversations will never go precisely as planned. Nevertheless, the key to the above is to start by **listening** and asking questions. Then, after offering some **reasoning**, you can **propose** more information for their consideration. However, I encourage you not to provide the long-winded paragraph response initially. It has a better chance of landing after you have listened to establish some trust and rapport.

As you read and reflect on your own conversations, you may develop your own unique questions to respond in different situations. I highly recommend writing them down![10]

In developing questions, I've found it helpful to use this question as a guide: *What questions can you ask to help someone see something that is worth seeing?* By beginning with the point that something is worth seeing, you can create a line of questioning to lead someone there. You can anticipate where he might resist and where your arguments can be strengthened. Over time, you'll have a wide array of questions you can use to respond to various issues.

Next, there is the **middlegame**. This frequently consists in diving into the details of specific arguments, evidence, and claims. Perhaps both you and your discussion partner can ask probing questions to find out more about the positions you hold. It also affords the opportunity to clarify misunderstandings that arose in the opening of the conversation.

In this book, I boil down the middlegame to arguments, principles, and examples. You should be able to offer an argument for your conversation partner's consideration. Also, you should know the underlying principles relevant to the slogan. Additionally, you want to have some clear examples to show that the principles are reasonable.

For example, in a middlegame discussion about the problem of evil, you might offer the point that we cannot see the whole picture when it comes to God's will and intentions, so there could be a good reason for him to permit a particular evil that we cannot discern. This being the case, we cannot conclude that the existence of evil implies that God does not exist.

To support the "we cannot see the whole picture" principle, we might offer the example of the so-called butterfly effect—the idea that a butterfly flapping its wings at a particular place and time can send a ripple effect through history, with massive implications that are indiscernible at the time of its flapping. This is an example of an argument, principle, and example of the type you will find in the middlegame section of each chapter.

Keep in mind, as we deploy the chess analogy, that I don't mean to reduce apologetics and evangelization to "just a game." Apologetics can be conceived of as an academic discipline11 or as a set of tools to assist in evangelization. Insofar as it bolsters the faith of believers, refutes the errors of unbelievers, or assists Catholics in the New Evangelization, it is *serious business.*

As my friend Pat Flynn likes to say, "Apologetics is not about winning arguments; it's about saving souls."[12] Of course, that does not mean that *we* save souls by doing apologetics, but it does imply that God can use us as instruments to bring the Holy Spirit into someone's life, and that one of the ways this can occur is through apologetics.

Neither do I want to reduce apologetic encounters to tactical procedures, strategies, and playbooks that fail to treat other persons as persons. John Nash's breakthroughs in game theory do not apply mechanically to conversations with those who differ on matters of faith and morals. People are influenced in all sorts of ways by all sorts of things, and our goal is to defuse some objections in an effort to lead them closer to Christ. Moreover, in following the first part of the **listen–reason–propose** schema, we have to **listen** to other persons, which requires treating them as people who deserve to be heard.

If we can help others see that their slogans do not succeed, we may have placed a pebble in their shoe. By God's grace this could be an important step in the conversion process. By no means should we expect that if we say A, B, and C, then they will say D, and we will say E, and then they will convert. People are not machines to be programmed or projects to be completed, but rather treasures made in the image of God, with all of the messiness you'd expect to find in a human being in a fallen world.

In his tactical chess manual, Silman spends considerable space on the *endgame* of achieving checkmate. What might that look like in an apologetics encounter? Maybe you're tempted to think it's immediate conversion and renouncement of atheism. But this is extremely unlikely!

People do not convert after one conversation. It can take many conversations and years of considering relevant issues, accompanied by prayer. Moreover, an openness and response to God's grace is required. There's a mystery of the interplay between the grace of faith and the free operation of the will, such that we should pray that God open the person up to receiving the grace of faith.

In chess, checkmate only occurs when your opponent *allows himself* to be checkmated. If someone storms out in rage or knocks over the pieces when he sees himself in a tough spot, no checkmate can take place. Instead, he must show honesty and maturity in allowing his opponent to make the final move, sealing his fate.

Similarly, in real-life apologetic conversations, your job is not to checkmate your opponent. He can always get up from the game and say he no longer wants to play. Rather, you should seek to lead him to the truth, and show him the reasonableness of faith. At most, you can put him in the right spot where he can allow himself to be checkmated by the Holy Spirit. If you think someone is close to that point, make an extra effort to pray for him.[13]

What about when you're stumped or in over your head? In certain cases, your conversation partner may be a well-studied atheist student of philosophy or history. He may raise objections or points that you have never heard. He may refer to sophisticated, scholarly arguments. A similar situation arises when an experienced chess player competes with an expert and feels overwhelmed. Let me offer three helpful tips related to this situation.

First, don't panic. Part of the reason we pray every day is to deepen our relationship with God and nourish our souls so that we cannot be tossed around by a challenge we can't answer in the moment.

Second, use the conversation as a chance to learn important facts or arguments. Ask **diagnostic questions** to ascertain precisely what the person is arguing. Compliment him for doing his homework and considering the issue at a deep level. Don't be afraid to say, "Wow, I've never heard that before or thought about that. Can you help me understand the details behind this point?" Later on, you might tell your discussion partner that you intend to think about the issue more and get back to him. This skeptic has just provided us motivation to deepen our faith, and that's a major good that can come out of an uncomfortable situation.

Third, realize that such interactions with studied philosophers and skeptics are not the norm. More often than not, the objections you hear will be one of the twenty slogans in this book. For those, I'm going to show you exactly how to answer them. Some slogans are more serious than others, and I will deal with them at greater length. Others are more superficial and can be tackled in just a few pages. Slogans one through nine constitute the first part of the book and proceed according to the following outline:

1. The Slogan
   a. What the slogan states or suggests
   b. Common versions of the slogan with sources
2. Openings
   a. Diagnostic and dialectical questions
   b. A discussion of the important questions to ask and why
3. Middlegame
   a. Arguments, principles, and examples
   b. The important principles at play and how to support them with examples
4. Summary & Resources
   a. Catalogue questions, arguments, principles, and examples
   b. Recommended resources for diving deeper into the objection

In slogans ten through twenty, I condense the opening and middlegame responses into one section. These chapters vary in length as needed to address slogans related to faith, evidence, and other concerns. Finally, I will offer some counsel on presenting evidence for God along with a number of useful arguments.

As a final note, I emphasize that the questions, principles, and examples I propose are not magic bullets. Apologetics and evangelization do not consist of cookie-cutter encounters. Rather, when you engage with people made in the image of God, the hope is twofold: 1) to bolster the faith of fellow Catholic Christians hearing the encounter, and 2) to bring atheists closer to embracing the one, true faith. Use the material in this book as a framework and a road map. **I aim to give you a detailed starting point for answering the slogans, sayings, and tropes that atheists use to challenge your faith.**

POPULAR SLOGANS

1

"There is no evidence for God's existence."

In a popular YouTube video with more than 275,000 views, Hemant Mehta provides "20 SHORT Arguments Against God's Existence."[14] The first argument he makes is to express emphatically, "There's no evidence." This is a common claim among internet atheists. The claim puts theists on the defensive while making atheists out to be the rational ones. The implication is that these atheists follow reason and evidence, whereas religious people have blind faith and no evidence. Let's respond carefully.

OPENING RESPONSES

Notice that the atheist makes a strong claim. In order for him to state confidently, "There is no evidence," you would expect that such a person went looking for evidence and found none. Sometimes, instead, the atheist may make a less sweeping claim, such as, "I've never seen any convincing evidence for God's existence." This more modest version of the slogan also implies that the person went searching for evidence at some point in his life. This, though, should ground our initial response.

Remember, whenever possible we want to ask questions rather than make statements. Start with a question that will reveal how much this atheist has studied. I learned this question from Trent Horn when he asked it effectively on *Catholic Answers Live*: **"What's the best evidence for God that you've heard and what do you think is wrong with it?"** I'll call this the "chapter one question," and we will refer back to it frequently in this book.

Trent points out that some atheists will refuse to answer this, since the concept of "best evidence" makes it sound like there is actual evidence, which they do not grant. If that happens to you, quickly update the question, **"What's the least bad evidence you've heard for God's existence and what do you think is wrong with it?"**[15]

In general, you will hear three different kinds of responses:

1. They've never heard of *any* evidence.
2. They've heard *vague, weak* evidence.
3. They've heard *strong evidence* but found flaws in the reasoning.

Let's address each case.

If the atheist has never heard *any evidence*, respond as follows:

"Really? You've never heard *any* evidence? I understand your atheism, then, because if there truly were no good reasons to believe in God, it's hard to see why one should believe. **But I think there *is* good evidence.** I can think of three or four pieces of evidence off the top of my head. Would you like to hear more about any of those?"

That shifts the conversation from the idea that there is no evidence for God to the actual arguments for him. Of course, this requires some preparation in studying the reasons to believe in God. The list in brackets can be tailored to your specific body of knowledge. I recommend including at least three arguments worthy of discussion. This reveals that there's not just one thing to consider but many avenues that people have found convincing.

Responding to 2): it's possible the atheist has only heard *vague or weak* evidence—claims that depend on subjective experience or unjustified premises. Some examples include:

- "My friend told me he prayed for a job after an interview and got the job."
- "If there's no God, then how'd we all get here?"
- "The world just seems to have design in it. When you look at flowers, they're really pretty, so to me, that shows God exists."
- "Sometimes you just gotta go with your gut. Since I was little, I've known in my heart that God is there."
- "Most people believe in God, so it just seems more reasonable to go with that big majority."

If a person refers to this sort of vague or weak evidence, respond as follows:

"You know, I'd have to agree that some evidence doesn't seem very strong at all. But I think there are better reasons to think that God exists. Have you ever considered [the contingency argument, the Kalam cosmological argument, the fine-tuning argument, the moral argument, etc.]?"

In that response you do two things. First, you affirm the person and find common ground in assessing some evidence as weak or vague. Second, you turn the discussion to stronger pieces of evidence. Again, the bracketed list can vary and be tailored to what you have studied the most.

Responding to 3): it's possible the atheist has heard some strong evidence but finds fault with it. He might say something like:

- "I've heard the contingency argument, but I think it commits the fallacy of *composition*. Just because parts of the universe are contingent, it doesn't mean the whole universe is contingent."
- "I've heard the fine-tuning argument, but I think the multiverse explanation is much more plausible than design. There could be so many universes that at least one just happens to be life-permitting by chance."
- "I've heard the moral argument, but I think it fails because moral philosophers have adequately grounded our moral beliefs in naturalistic ways."

If that's how your conversation partner responds, you should do three things. First, compliment the person for doing his homework. By actually looking into at least one argument, this skeptic reveals a willingness to look at evidence for God. Second, clarify the objection by asking questions. Make sure you understand what he has in mind with the fine-tuning argument, contingency argument, and so forth. A simple follow-up will do: **"Can you explain that objection in more detail?"**

Third, show why his objection doesn't defeat the argument. This may not be easy, and you may not be able to provide an answer on the spot. But if you have done your homework, and you know how to respond, then do it like this:

"That's an interesting objection, and I think it's great that you've taken the time to look into that argument. Have you ever considered [*insert response to his objection*]?"

This drives the conversation back to the evidence and arguments. Perhaps you can give this atheist more food for thought regarding whether there are good reasons to believe in God. At the very least, the hope is that he will trust you as someone willing to have rational dialogue. In the future, he'll be less likely to sling slogans at you or take an aggressive tone.

In the case that you do not know how to defuse the objection, you can admit that honestly. You might say, **"That's a really interesting objection, and I think it's great that you've taken the time to look into that argument. Would it be all right if I look into this a bit more and get back to you?"**

Then, do you your homework and get back to him! Atheists who are willing to look into the arguments honestly should be given clear answers to their objections.

MIDDLEGAME RESPONSES

Recall that the point of the middlegame section is to provide arguments, principles, and examples to assist you as the conversation moves past its opening stages. In this chapter, I encourage you to keep your eye on three different principles at play when someone claims, "There's no evidence for God."

Principle 1: Claiming there's no evidence is not the same as showing there's no evidence.

It's a bold claim to assert there is no evidence for something. It implies that the one asserting it has done a considerable amount of searching and found *nothing*. At some point in the conversation, you may need to point this out. A simple example can do the trick.

Suppose someone asserted, "There's no evidence that Einstein's general theory of relativity is true." What would follow from this? Precisely nothing. Just because someone *said* there's no evidence for Einstein's general theory does not mean there actually *is* no evidence for Einstein's general theory. Rather, the person would have to show that he has looked into the proposed evidence and that none of it is any good. Similarly, if someone asserts there is no evidence for God (and wants this assertion to be taken seriously), he will need to show he has looked into proposed evidence and that none of it is any good.

Principle 2: Scientific evidence is not the only type of evidence.

Sometimes, people modify the slogan and say, "There is no scientific evidence for God" or "God's existence has never been empirically demonstrated." This carries weight, since people have come to appreciate the scientific method as an effective way of finding truth. But just because one way is highly effective does not imply that there are no other effective ways of finding truth.

Edward Feser provides the following example.16 Suppose you have an extremely effective metal detector. You bring it to the beach in the hope of finding plastic cups. You search and search with the metal detector, but you never find any such cups. Should you then infer that there are no plastic cups on that beach? Of course not. Metal detectors are not a reliable tool for finding plastic cups.

Similarly, God, as traditionally understood, is not a physical thing that can be found under a microscope or through telescopes. Rather, he is the immaterial, necessary creator of all things, and cannot be found through empirical methods of investigating material realities. In other words, saying that God doesn't exist because he cannot be detected by scientific instruments is like saying plastic cups don't exist since they cannot be detected by metal detectors.

So what other sources of evidence are there besides modern science? Philosophy has been the domain of arguments for God's existence for millennia. It can be thought of as the pursuit of wisdom and knowledge using intellectual tools. So although philosophers might make use of the results of scientific experiments, common human experience, and historical considerations, primarily they *reason* to general conclusions from principles we grasp with our intellects.

One of the quickest ways to see that scientific experiments are insufficient in finding all truths is to consider *ethics*. When discussing how we should or should not act, we cannot make conclusions based on dials in a laboratory. Philosophical principles related to the nature of human beings and human action must be considered and applied.

The person asserting that there is no evidence for God typically holds a narrow view about what constitutes evidence. Ask, **"What do you mean by** *evidence*?**"** If he asserts that evidence must be empirical or subject to the scientific method, then you can proceed as previously described by showing that's not the only way of finding truth. Use a question to encourage your interlocutor to be open to evidence from philosophy or history. Ask, **"Shouldn't we be open-minded toward** *all* **evidence? Even if it's philosophical or historical?"** I revisit this issue in chapter three, when we discuss particular scientific objections.

Principle 3: The quality of evidence is not to be judged on how swiftly it persuades someone.

Many people expect arguments for God's existence to work like knockdown magic that overwhelms a person and instantly converts him. That expectation colors how people see the evidence. Some think that if the person is not immediately bulldozed, the arguments must not be any good.

But the strength of an argument should be judged by objective criteria (well-supported premises, valid reasoning, and so forth), not by how many people it swiftly persuades. Would Einstein's general relativity theory be false just because arguments for it failed to convince a layman in under two minutes? Certainly not. Similarly, when it comes to arguments for God's existence, people may throw up barriers that prevent them from reasoning to the conclusion. One of those barriers is the thought that other people do not find the arguments convincing. But one should not let this thought stop them from considering the full range of evidence for a particular view.

At this point, a helpful example you could provide would be something that you changed your mind about after investigating the evidence. This will be different for all of us. But if there's an issue or event that you used to think about the same way as most people, but then changed your mind, that will be useful to show the importance of looking into the evidence. But you must also exercise prudence, since if the example in view is highly controversial, then that issue itself will likely become the main topic of conversation.

A personal example relates to how I viewed the American Civil War. I once had a very superficial understanding that went something like this: *slavery was bad, and the heroic Union launched a war to free the slaves from the evil Confederacy.* But after learning more of the history, I came to see that the time period was a lot more complicated and the South's claims more nuanced. After weighing more evidence, I saw that my simplistic picture of the Civil War and its causes could no longer stand up to scrutiny. Though I still viewed slavery as immoral, I no longer viewed the North as all good and the South as all bad.

Select your own example to make this point. It's possible to hold a view, investigate the evidence, and later come to revise that view. Just because other people have a particular viewpoint, it should not bar anyone from examining the evidence in search of the truth.

By following the strategy of listen, reason, and propose, you can make considerable progress in a conversation with a skeptic who says there's no evidence for God.

Questions to Ask

- "What's the best evidence you've heard and what do you think is wrong with it?"
- "If you had to choose, what evidence for God is the least bad?"
- "What do you mean by evidence?"
- "Shouldn't we be open to all kinds of evidence?"

Middlegame Principles

- Claiming that there is no evidence is not the same as showing there is no evidence.
- Scientific evidence is not the only type of evidence.
- The quality of evidence is not based on how swiftly it persuades someone.

Resources for Further Study

- Watch this high-quality video produced by *Capturing*

Christianity, which responds to the slogan, "There's no evidence for God's existence" https://www.youtube.com/watch?v=0XES1c60AXM.

- Read Trent Horn's book *Answering Atheism* for a good survey of theistic arguments.
- See the arguments for God's existence in appendix B.

2

"I just believe in one less God than you do."

This New Atheist slogan has been made popular by the comedian Ricky Gervais and the biologist Richard Dawkins. Gervais deployed this slogan in an interview with Stephen Colbert,17 and Richard Dawkins opens his book *Outgrowing God* with an extended version:

> I don't believe in any of the hundreds and hundreds of sky gods, river gods, sea gods, sun gods, star gods, moon gods, weather gods, fire gods, forest gods . . . So many gods to not believe in. And I don't believe in Yahweh, the God of the Jews. But it's quite likely you do, if you were brought up a Jew, a Christian, or a Muslim.[18]

Joe Rogan interviewed Dawkins about the book and remarked that this line of argument is a "home run."[19]

The main argument works like this. Christians believe in one God, but they *disbelieve* in *thousands* of gods (from non-Christian religions). One might say they are atheists with respect to all those other gods. Well, the atheist just goes "one god further" in rejecting the Christian God, too. Unlike believers who are basically selective atheists, nonbelievers are fully consistent atheists. They apply the logic of disbelief to all proposed gods rather than making one weird exception.

Dawkins intertwines this slogan with a geographical one: "If you were born in Saudi Arabia, you'd be a Muslim." Put that aside for a moment, but in chapter eighteen we'll address it.

OPENING RESPONSES

Let's begin with some questions and listening. Ask questions to get at the idea that finite gods of various cultures are not in the same category as the creator-God of traditional monotheism. Consider the following questions:

- Do you think all those gods are the same? If so, can you explain more?
- What do you mean by "god"?
- What are some of the differences in those types of gods you mention?

Now, your discussion partner might insist that they are all the same in that there's *no evidence* for any of them! If that's the case, I refer you back to chapter one and the "no evidence" slogan. After that, we should turn to a more fundamental point.

In an article titled "Why I Believe in One More God Than the Atheists," Pat Flynn provides a helpful illustration to see a major flaw in the slogan:

> With respect to the "one less god" objection, there is not much respect that ought to be given to it, quite frankly. A crime is committed. One hundred people come under suspicion. We evaluate the evidence and conclude only one of them is the perpetrator. The atheist with respect

to criminality, clutching his copy of *Skeptic* magazine, objects with a self-satisfied grin: "Listen, fellas, I only believe in one less criminal than you. Why not let them all go?" Nobody takes such a person seriously. And nobody should.[20]

As Flynn explains, just because many gods are fictional, it does not follow that there is no creator-God. Viewing the slogan in the best light, the atheist is making an inductive inference. That is, he reasons from several supposedly similar cases to another one. But the inference fails for two reasons:

1. He has not shown *how* those other gods are similar to each other or to the God of traditional monotheism.[21] Before making the inference, the atheist must explain how the God of traditional monotheism is just like Zeus or Thor (or whatever god he wants to mention).

2. Creation implies a creator, even if he's been misidentified in the past. Various features of our world, such as the contingency of things, motion, moral facts, and the fine-tuning of the universe, form the basis of arguments for God's existence.

There's another, someone what obvious opening option when someone says, "I believe in one less God than you do," suggested by Christian apologist Greg Koukl: "Yes, that's true, and that's what makes you an atheist and me a theist." Naturally the conversation can then turn to *why* you hold your respective positions. Then you can follow up, **"Why do you believe atheism is true?"** or ask the Trent Horn question, **"What's the best evidence for God that you've heard and what do you think is wrong with it?"**

MIDDLEGAME RESPONSES

Let's highlight two principles that will help you to make the fundamental issues clear in a conversation that begins with this slogan.

Principle 1: A lack of evidence for *some* gods does not mean there is no evidence for *any* gods.

To make this clear, provide an illustration. Here's one. Suppose a wealthy lady has her diamond necklace stolen right off her neck. The thief disappeared into the crowd so swiftly and smoothly that she caught no glimpse of him. Let's say the police search the parade and question a thousand suspects but none are found to be the thief. Would this imply that *there is no thief?* Of course, that's ridiculous.

From the fact that a thousand suspects turn up innocent, it does not follow that there is no guilty party. Similarly, just because thousands of gods are found to be fictional, it does not follow that God does not exist. Also, my usage of "god" and "God" serves to safeguard a distinction between finite gods and the infinite God of classical theism. More on that in a moment.

At this stage, our main criticism of the slogan has been that it does not prove much of anything at all. Even if there is no good reason to believe in Poseidon or Athena, it does not follow that there is no reason to believe in a transcendent creator.

Principle 2: The God of classical theism is not like the finite, mutable gods of other religions.

The many "sky gods, sea gods, river gods, and sun gods" to which Professor Dawkins refers, as well as the many gods of mythologies, are finite and mutable. They are properly referred to as "gods" with a lowercase *g*. For example, we frequently find the gods of mythology eating, procreating, wooing mortals, and battling one another. These descriptions imply that such gods are in many ways just like we are.

But if that is so, a question remains, **"Where did all these gods come from?"** In other words, none of them is the transcendent creator of finite reality upon which all creatures depend for their existence. They are more or less like us with more and better powers.

In those important respects they are unlike the God of classical monotheism. In thinking of God, uppercase G, as god, lowercase g, the atheist has made a critical category mistake. The God of classical monotheism is the infinite, eternal, unchangeable, creator of all that exists. As the great twentieth-century Dominican Fr. Herbert McCabe put it:

> What God accounts for is that the universe is there instead of nothing. I have said that whatever God is, he is not a member of everything, not an inhabitant of the universe, not a thing or kind of thing. . . . We come across God, so to speak, or rather we search and do *not* come across him, when the universe itself raises for us a radical question concerning its existence at all. And creation is the name we give to God's answering this question.[22]

We can see from this description that the God of classical theism transcends our categories in a way that is much different from the finite, mutable gods of mythology. Keep in mind that in this chapter we did not prove God's existence. Rather, we laid down important questions and principles you can use to address the slogan, "I believe in one less god than you do."

When atheists tell Christians, "You are also an atheist, because you don't believe in all these other gods; I just believe in one less than God than you," that's like a bachelor telling a married man, "You are also a bachelor because you aren't married to all these other women; I'm just married to one less woman than you."[23]

43

This bachelor mistakenly thinks the married man is an inconsistent bachelor who rejects nearly all women but arbitrarily chooses one to marry. In reality, a married man chooses no longer to be a bachelor because he sees marriage to one woman is *superior* to marrying any other woman or simply not marrying any woman. Likewise, the Christian believes in the God of classical theism because believing in this God is superior to believing in any other "gods" or simply not believing in any God when it comes to proposing an ultimate explanation of the world.

Questions to Ask

- "What do you mean by god?"
- "Do you think all of those gods are the same? If not, how are they different?"
- "Does the existence of counterfeit money mean that there's no real money?"[24]
- "What do you think of this scenario. Someone commits a crime of vandalism. A dozen people come under suspicion, yet they all are exonerated. Should the police stop looking for a criminal? Is it possible there is no criminal?"
- "Have you ever considered that creation points to a creator even if he's been misidentified or misunderstood in other contexts?"

Middlegame Principles

- A lack of evidence for some gods does not entail there is no evidence for *any* god.

- The God of classical theism is not like the finite, mutable gods of other religions.

Recommendations for Further Study

- Trent Horn answers the objection in a short YouTube video: https://www.youtube.com/watch?v=SHlnEQPSWFM.
- Pat Flynn's article addresses this objection and more: https://www.wordonfire.org/resources/blog/why-i-believe-in-one-more-god-than-the-atheists/24628/.

3

"I don't believe in God because I believe in science."

According to many twenty-first-century skeptics, when it comes to truth, science has the final say. The belief that science and religion are at war, often called the "conflict thesis," is part of the air we breathe, and is embodied in the slogan: I don't believe in God; I believe in science.

Believers must share some of the blame for this. There's no doubt some were told in Sunday school to stop asking questions. Part of our motivation for answering atheistic slogans should be to reveal the intellectual side of religious ideas, since great minds like St. Augustine and St. Thomas Aquinas have been doing this for thousands of years.

This slogan comes in other varieties, such as, "science has disproved God."

Ultimately, this slogan is an assertion of the conflict thesis: that there is a war between science and religion and everyone must choose a side. Since it's only an assertion, we need to probe deeper to find out the reasons why a person holds to it. Let's dive in.

OPENING RESPONSES

Start with a question of clarification: **"What precisely is the incompatibility you see between believing in God and believing in science?"**

Or if the person has asserted, "science has disproved God," then you want to ask, **"When and how has science disproved God?"**

Both versions of these first questions ask the objector to tell us more. That's what we want. Questions allow you to gather information so that your response can be more appropriate and effective.

Before you go making assertions that rebut this person's claims, you need to find what exactly he has in mind. Typically, people just repeat what they've heard, and they think Christians can't believe in science.

They're not right, and this question will force atheists to clarify their position. Usually, they have one of five ideas in mind when making this objection:

1. Evolution contradicts the creation stories in the Bible.

2. There's no scientific evidence for God.

3. Miracles are impossible.

4. Neuroscience has disproved the soul.

5. Most scientists are atheists.

Prepare to respond to each one in turn and show how none of these issues demonstrate an irresolvable conflict between faith and science.

1. "Evolution contradicts the Creation stories in the Bible."

This slogan presupposes that evolution cannot fit into a theistic worldview. First, point out that evolution and the existence of God are not mutually exclusive. God *could* have created the living things of the world through some long process of "evolution" if he wanted to do that. There's a robust debate on this issue (with faithful Catholics on all sides) and the scientific arguments are beyond our scope here, but the key point can be made simply by asking, **"Have you considered that it's possible to believe in both God and evolution?"**

Another point we can make: Catholics are not strict biblical literalists like some Fundamentalist Protestants. We recognize a variety of genres within the biblical texts. There is no requirement to take every text in the Bible literally. The Catholic Church teaches in the *Catechism* that the creation stories contain truths about God and the world, yet convey them with figurative language. For example, in CCC 390 it reads:

> The account of the fall in Genesis 3 uses figurative language, but affirms a primeval event, a deed that took place at the beginning of the history of man. Revelation gives us the certainty of faith that the whole of human history is marked by the original fault freely committed by our first parents.

Press the objector with another question, **"Why can't God and evolution coexist in your view? Why must it be one or the other?"** Even if you are not sold on evolution yourself, this question will help your discussion partner see that God's existence is compatible with biological evolution. So, the theory of evolution is not a good reason to be an atheist.

2. "There's no scientific evidence for God."

This slogan presupposes *scientism*: the position that the methods of science provide the only way of obtaining real knowledge. If God cannot be shown to exist by empirical science, then there cannot be any real evidence for God.

But scientism faces at least two devastating problems: 1) it is self-defeating, and 2) there are other ways of coming to know truth. It is self-defeating because the claim that science is the only way of obtaining real knowledge is not itself knowledge obtained through the scientific method. You might ask a scientism advocate, **"What experiments have shown that science is the only way of obtaining real knowledge?"** There is no coherent answer to such a question. The bottom line is that scientism is a *philosophical* position, not a scientific one.

Consider other truths arrived at independently of scientific studies. These include truths of logic, mathematics, metaphysics, ethics, aesthetics, and historical studies. Of course, science can inform some of those areas of study, but each contains truths that are arrived at independently of the scientific method.

So even if there is no scientific evidence for God, that does not show atheism is true, since science is not the only way of obtaining real knowledge. Refer back to the metal detector illustration in chapter one for another helpful illustration you can incorporate into your response.

3. "Miracles are impossible."

One might hear several variations of this slogan, such as, "science has shown that miracles do not occur," or "miracles are physically impossible according to the laws of nature."

These assertions reveal a commitment to naturalism as a worldview. Broadly, we might define naturalism as the view that everything arises from natural causes, thus excluding supernatural explanations. In other words, there is no God or anything like God, and the final explanations of reality are ultimately physical in nature. Of course, *if* naturalism is true, then miracles are impossible. But if naturalism is *not* true, then miracles could occur.

At this stage, the theist can point out that *if* God exists, then of course he can work a miracle. In other words, God can suspend laws of nature in special circumstances to bring about a specific outcome. If the atheist thinks that *not even God* can do this, he owes us an explanation as to why that is. Let's make these points clear to our conversation partner by asking, **"Would you agree that if God exists, he could perform a miracle? And if not, why not?"**

In all likelihood, he will agree that God could perform a miracle if he existed, but will assert that God *doesn't* exist. But this only shows that the supposed impossibility of miracles is not proof of atheism; it merely depends on atheism being true.

At this point, the skeptic might make one of the following new claims: 1) scientists can't assume miracles are possible when working in the lab; this would undermine their ability to confirm or disconfirm experimental hypotheses; and 2) no miracles have ever been demonstrated.

These claims do not bolster skepticism. As for 1), it merely reveals a methodological commitment as opposed to an ontological commitment. In other words, scientists do not look for miracles as part of the scientific method, but this methodological choice does not imply there are no miracles in reality. To think otherwise would be akin to saying that choosing not to look for items smaller than two inches demonstrates that no items smaller than two inches exist. Moreover, on the Catholic Christian worldview, miracles are very rare events, and this rarity makes the methodological commitment appropriate even for Catholic scientists.

As far as 2) is concerned, it depends on what someone means by "demonstrated." Miracle claims occur around the globe, and many indeed claim to have verifiable evidence that a miracle has taken place. These claims are documented and assessed in various works.[25] Regardless, even if no miracle had ever been demonstrated to the skeptic's satisfaction, that would not mean God does not exist. At most, it would show that God has done no miracles that would satisfy the skeptic. But it would not follow from that that God does not exist or even that God has worked no miracles.

So even these additional claims fail to show an irresolvable conflict between believing in God and believing in science. If God exists, he can work a miracle, and atheists cannot prove otherwise.

4. "Neuroscience has disproved the soul."

This sub-slogan comes with certain assumptions. Religious people believe in souls inside of our bodies that make up our true identity. This free-floating, cloud-like substance they call the "soul" does not actually exist. Neuroscience has advanced to the point where we can pinpoint the location of brain activity that corresponds with all of our thoughts and actions. No science-oriented person can still believe in a soul.

Before getting into the soul issue, you might ask the person, **"What exactly do you have in mind and how does this relate to God's existence?"** After all, even if neuroscience succeeded in showing we have nothing like a soul in any sense, that would not show that God doesn't exist. Remember the dialectical context: your discussion partner has proposed this neuroscience objection as a reason why he does not believe in God. Yet the most this objection might show is that God did not make human beings in the way many people think he did.[26] Nonetheless, this diagnostic question allows you to gather information and see how your conversation partner is thinking. Next, you can dig further into their understanding of the soul.

Ask, **"What exactly do you mean by soul?"** Also, **"How precisely has neuroscience disproved the soul?"** Listen carefully to the answers. The chances are, the proponent of this objection will stick to a model of the soul as some sort of ectoplasmic substance. Follow up with another question, **"Have you considered that some people might think about the soul in different ways?"** That question plants a seed. Although particular models of the soul may seem less plausible in the wake of neuroscience, that does not imply all models of the soul are implausible.

At this point, you might explain a more Catholic understanding of the soul. Traditionally, Catholics, drawing upon Aristotle, have held that the soul is the *form* of the body, its unifying and animating principle. It is that which makes the difference between a person who is alive and one who is dead. In this sense, all living creatures have some sort of soul. Plants have a *vegetative* soul, dogs and cats have an *animal* soul, and human beings have *rational* souls.

In other words, they each have a *formative principle* from which flow various operations. Understanding the soul in this sense, we can see that science has not disproved the soul. That's because it's not the type of thing that can be seen through neurosurgery or brain scans. We might see bodily activity correlated with various thoughts and actions, but not a philosophical principle that gives rise to our intellectual operations.[27]

Another way of getting at your conception of the soul is with an illustration.[28] Suppose Jeff wants to see Brown University. He drives there and takes a college tour. The tour guide shows him various academic buildings, the student center, the cafeteria, a freshman dorm, and some athletic facilities. After the tour is over, Jeff says, "Thank you very much, but when are you going to show us the university?" The tour guide stares at Jeff with bewilderment.

Jeff conceives of "the university" as one building among many, and he is surprised that he has not seen it yet. In Jeff's mind, the tour guide has showed him many different places on campus, but not "the university." However, the problem is that Jeff has misconceived what "Brown University" actually is. It's not one building or single place on a campus. Rather, it's that which unifies various buildings, classes, faculty members, and students for purposes of higher education. It's an organization of higher education.

From the fact that Jeff has not seen the university in the sense in which he misconceived it (as one more building alongside the others), it does not follow that Brown University does not exist. Similarly, from the fact that neuroscience does not locate the soul in the way some people misconceive it (e.g., as a ghostly substance that floats in our heads), it does not follow that we do not have souls.

Your friend might press, **"But why not just call it the brain? Why use the words *mind* or *soul* at all? Everything just occurs in the brain, and neuroscience confirms this."** Here, you might point out that even if everything he said is correct, it would not give a good reason for rejecting God.

Theism does not require belief in a soul whose activity does not closely correlate with brain or bodily functions. Like a talented pianist's performance is tightly correlated with the keys of the piano, the soul is tightly correlated with brain activity. Yet, the pianist *transcends* the piano keys, as he is not reducible to them, just as the soul in particular aspects transcends the brain.[29] We might sum this up with the principle: tight correlation between X and Y does not entail that X is reducible to Y or that Y alone exists.

In this way, you can accept both neuroscience *and* God. This sub-slogan does not support the original slogan, "I don't believe in God; I believe in science," since it does not show that believing in neuroscience is incompatible with believing in God.

Also, you can agree with your friend's point generally: **"You're right that the brain is the organ where our cognition takes place. Our *embodied* cognition certainly requires use of the brain (that's what makes it based on bodily functions). But, as I've explained, that does nothing to show there is not a soul, understood as the *form* of the body, a principle that animates living human beings."**

Now, there are aspects of our cognition that cannot be explained purely by brain processes. But we will not go into the details of that here. I will refer you to some more detailed presentations in the recommended reading at the end of the chapter.

5. "Most scientists are atheists."

The person making this assertion probably has a statistic to back it up. But we should still ask for his sources. Perhaps he will respond by noting that 93 percent of the scientists in the National Academy of Sciences do not believe in God.

Trent Horn points out[30] that this is only a small fraction of professional scientists. The Pew Research Center found that about half of scientists believe in God or a "higher power" in a 2009 study.[31] So at best, it is unclear that the great majority of scientists are atheists.

As part of your response, you may find it helpful to mention the Society of Catholic Scientists.[32] This organization has hundreds of Catholic scientists with Ph.D.'s in different fields. Moreover, they have strict requirements for membership, as can be found on their website:

> Regular members must have earned a Ph.D. or the equivalent in a natural science, and have one or more of the following: a) a currently active research program at a college, university, or recognized research facility such as a government or industry laboratory, b) a faculty teaching position in a science department at a college or university, c) a distinguished record of service to science at the national or international level. Individuals who have retired from the field after a distinguished career in research, teaching, and/or service may also be considered for regular membership.[33]

So even if there are many scientists who are atheists, there are also many scientists who are Catholic. Additionally, we might point to the many Catholic scientists in history, both laymen and clergy, who made major contributions to their fields, such as Gregor Mendel or George Lemaitre, two Catholic priests who made revolutionary discoveries in genetics and cosmology, respectively.

But even if it were true that the vast majority of scientists are atheists (which, as we've seen, there is reason to question) it would not follow that atheism is true.

We might ask, "What does the fact that most scientists are atheists prove? It seems like you're saying people who study science are very smart, and since their scientific studies led them to atheism we should follow their lead. But if that's the case, shouldn't we examine whatever *reasons* led them to atheism and not just be impressed by the fact that they are atheists?"

Also, instead of science making these people atheists, what if atheism just made them more likely to become scientists? If that's true, then why not just consider their opinions to be the same as other regular people who think about this issue and not give it some special authority?"[34]

After all, scientists are no more qualified to be the arbiters of the truth about God than economists. Rather, we should look to philosophy and theology for the most persuasive and pertinent arguments for God's existence. In other words, instead of conceding our interlocutor's assumption that scientists are uniquely competent to pronounce on the subject of God, we should encourage him to look to the *good reasons* offered by philosophers and theologians for why God exists and see if they hold up.

MIDDLEGAME RESPONSES

When attempting to show conflict between faith and science, the atheist often attempts to craft a narrative with multiple ideas. He might weave multiple slogans from the five points discussed above into a paragraph-long diatribe:

I don't believe in God, because I believe in science. There's a reason most scientists are atheists. They have examined the world carefully and study it on a daily basis, and guess what? They haven't found any evidence for God. They've found that evolution explains human origins without God. They've found out that the world operates according to laws of physics and chemistry.

There are no angels or ghosts running around in it. There's nothing supernatural. There's just rock-bottom physical reality. Of course, that might make some people uncomfortable, but it's the truth. People do not have souls and neuroscientists have shown this clearly. Instead of focusing on mythical, magical thinking in religion, we should stick to science that improves our technology and our lives.

In such a situation, it's typically ineffective to engage in dueling diatribes or respond with a line-by-line critique. Instead, ask some good questions to get at one or two foundational problems with the conflict thesis. You might respond, **"As a Catholic, I definitely value science. Can you specify the incompatibility you see between believing in God and believing in science? Why can't we do both?"** That will get the conversation moving and perhaps reveal which of the five areas your discussion partner finds most problematic. After that, you also want to remember some important principles.

Principle 1: Apparent incompatibility does not imply real incompatibility.

The example of evolution supports this general point. Some people might think Christianity is intellectually bankrupt because it demands believing in a special creation of every species (or other things, like a "young Earth," that most modern science disputes). To them, science and Christianity are apparently incompatible. However, once it's explained that Christianity does not demand that, the incompatibility evaporates. For a long time, Catholic Christians have defended the compatibility of evolution with the doctrine of creation. If God chose to create human beings at the end of a long process of evolution, that is his prerogative. So evolution and creation are not *really* incompatible.

In fact, Christians are free to follow scientific evidence where it leads, but for atheists, evolution and its materialistic assumptions are really the only game in town, and the theory must be adamantly defended no matter what. It may or may not be fitting to make that point with your conversation partner. Regardless, you can use one of several examples to show that apparent incompatibility does not mean real incompatibility.

Principle 2: Natural theology is a branch of philosophy, not natural science.

This principle addresses the issue behind the claim, "There's no scientific evidence for God." As the quote from Fr. Herbert McCabe illustrates, this is not surprising when we consider that the God of classical monotheism is not an item inside the universe or even one "god" among a pantheon of deities. Rather, he is the infinite, eternal, simple, transcendent creator of the entire created order.

As such, we should not expect to find evidence for God under the microscope or through a telescope. He's not tinier than an amoeba or farther than a distant galaxy—he's what is responsible for there being an amoeba or galaxy in the first place. We flush out some of these details of this later when we walk through a contingency argument in appendix B. For now, it suffices to point out that God is not a *thing* inside our universe So when we don't find God through scientific investigation we cannot conclude that he does not exist.

Instead, we must look to philosophy for our reasons to think God exists; specifically, to natural theology. The "natural" in natural theology refers to the fact that the natural theologian does not use supernatural revelation to investigate God, but rather facts and features of the natural world, including the discoveries of the empirical sciences. But he is not *restricted* to these things. He can make use of the full range of intellectual resources, which includes metaphysical arguments.

So the slogans attempting to show incompatibility between science and religion have no real force. As Pope John Paul II famously said, "Faith and reason are like two wings on which the human spirit rises to the contemplation of truth."[35] As Catholic Christians, we can be confident that true science and true religion cannot be in *real* conflict. All apparent conflicts can be resolved. Use the points of this chapter to help your friend who thinks it's impossible to believe in both God and science.

Questions to Ask

- "What precisely is the incompatibility between believing in God and believing in science?"
- "When and how did science disprove God?"
- Prepare replies to five apparent conflicts between science and religion:
  - Evolution shows the Bible is wrong about creation. **Answer:** Whatever the actual scientific merits of different evolution theories, in principle Christians can agree that it's possible for God to have created life on earth through an evolutionary process. A proper reading of Genesis does not rule that out.
  - There's no scientific evidence for God. **Answer:** Scientific evidence is not the only form of evidence and science is not the only way of knowing.
  - Miracles are not possible according to science. **Answer:** If God exists, then he can perform miracles. When doing experiments, scientists work on natural

phenomena, and as a methodological decision may exclude any supernatural explanation. However, this does not disprove the existence of nonphysical realities. Metal detectors cannot find plastic cups.

- Neuroscience has disproved the soul. **Answer:** No, it hasn't. The soul as traditionally understood in the Catholic tradition is not a ghostly substance, but rather the form of the body. As a spiritual, immaterial principle that animates the body, it cannot be detected by neuroscience. Additionally, particular aspects of cognition reveal immaterial operations of the rational soul.

- Most scientists are atheists. **Answer:** That's not entirely clear. In a 2009 Pew Research Center study, about half of the scientists said they believed in God or a higher power. Also, we should look to the domain of philosophy for the most relevant arguments related to God's existence. Scientists may not be qualified to examine theistic arguments.

Middlegame Principles

- Apparent incompatibility does not imply real incompatibility.
- Natural theology is a branch of philosophy, not natural science.

Recommended Resources

- Read the booklet *20 Answers: Faith and Science* by Trent Horn.

- Read the book *Particles of Faith* by Stacy Trasancos.
- Listen to this podcast episode with J.P. Moreland for a refutation of scientism: http://www.classicaltheism.com/JP.
- Watch this YouTube presentation by Edward Feser for a defense of the immateriality of the intellect: https://www.youtube.com/watch?v=w6GmCyKylTw.

4

"Extraordinary claims require extraordinary evidence."

In a recent exchange with skeptic John Loftus, Trent Horn encountered this slogan firsthand. Loftus raised it as one of his first arguments in their discussion on whether it's rational to believe in miracles, saying, "The central claims of the book are summed up in my chapter 'Extraordinary Claims Require Extraordinary Evidence.' The testimonial evidence is not enough to overcome what we experience every single day of our lives, every hour of the day, that miracles don't happen."[36]

A person might say by way of illustration, "Listen, if you told me you found a squirrel in your garage, then I'd probably believe you. But if you told me you found a fire-breathing dragon in your garage, I'd be highly skeptical. Why? Because extraordinary claims require extraordinary evidence."

This slogan exhibits threefold power in conversation. First, it sounds commonsensical and intelligent. Second, it instills anxiety in the believer, who might think: Shoot, unless I come up with extraordinary evidence, there's no way I can persuade this person. Third, it implicitly sets up a rule that rational people, as opposed to gullible or superstitious ones, must follow.

Solid preparation provides the remedy for slogans. Let's dive in and see how we can answer, "Extraordinary claims require extraordinary evidence."

OPENING RESPONSES

The atheist using this slogan has not set out to show that God does not exist. Rather, it allows him to harbor a sweeping skepticism regarding religious claims, specifically about miracles. In the middlegame section of this chapter, I examine the terms of the slogan in detail and offer responses. Here, I'll briefly suggest an opening response.

Since the slogan targets miraculous claims only and not God's existence generally, we might ask, **"That's an interesting point you make. I'm curious: Could it be true that extraordinary claims require extraordinary evidence *and* that God still exists?"** This small point has large ramifications.

In the previous three chapters, each slogan attempted to bring out a reason *not* to believe in God. Chapter one considered the idea of there being "no evidence." Chapter two dealt with the claim that we should believe in "one less god." Chapter three responded to the idea that we cannot believe in both God and science.

Here, the slogan's target is smaller. Rather than proposing a reason for atheism, it targets miraculous claims. Yet it should be clear that believing in the possibility of miracles depends on whether a person believes in God. These points may lead nicely into our chapter one question, **"What's the best evidence for God that you've heard and what do you think is wrong with it?"**

MIDDLEGAME RESPONSES

Is the slogan true? Do extraordinary claims require extraordinary evidence? It seems preposterous to suggest it might be false. Do we dare say extraordinary claims *don't* require extraordinary evidence? The atheist may say that's as crazy as believing a friend who says he has a dragon in his garage.

Principle 1: Clarify the terms of the slogan to probe its force.

On some definitions of the terms, the slogan turns out to be true, but on other definitions it turns out to be false. To judge whether the slogan is true, we must examine the terminology in detail. "Extraordinary claims" and "Extraordinary evidence" sound like impressive phrases, but we have to carefully define terms. So, ask the skeptic what he means.

You might say, **"What do you mean by *extraordinary* claims?"** The skeptic will likely answer one of two ways. Here's the first one:

1. Extraordinary claims involve extremely rare or improbable events.

Rarity, in and of itself, gives no reason to doubt a claim. It would be a rare event for your best friend to win the lottery, but if you had good reasons to think he did, you would not need to doubt it. For example, if you saw the winning ticket or the large check sent to him from the state, that would make it completely rational to believe your friend won the lottery. Next, let's consider a second possible answer.

2. Extraordinary claims involve the supernatural.

This reveals the true nature of the debate and the fundamental point we made in our opening response. Our worldview (e.g., classical theism, polytheism, atheism) dictates how we judge evidence. The atheist believes that supernatural events require extraordinary evidence because he believes that God does not exist, whereas the classical theist considers extraordinary events to be rare but live options because of God's power to work miracles.

You might ask, **"If God exists, is an event like raising Jesus from the dead really so extraordinary? It may be rare, but surely it's something the divine creator could bring about, right?"** The obvious answer is yes. If they say no and assert that not even God can do that, then we are not talking about the same God. If God exists, God can do a miracle. So, the question knocks the discussion back a step.[37]

In other words, if we have good reasons to think God exists, then supernatural events can be examined in a way similar to the lottery case. Yes, they may be rare, but if we have good evidence to believe they occurred, we can rationally affirm them.[38] We should not rule them out for lack of "extraordinary evidence."

A third possibility may emerge during the conversation:

3. Extraordinary claims involve rare or supernatural events *and* dramatically impact one's life choices.

This extra condition sometimes arises when discussing the meaning of "extraordinary evidence," so we will respond to this variation below.

Let's consider the next part of the slogan and ask, **"What do you mean by *extraordinary* evidence?"** Consider a couple of potential replies.

1. Extraordinary evidence is evidence that overcomes the exceedingly low intrinsic probability of an event.

What does it mean for an event to be "intrinsically" improbable? Scholars debate the best interpretations of probability, but let's stick with the commonsense notion that it seems highly unlikely the event would occur. But, proceeding along those lines, we find that good, ordinary evidence can be sufficient to overcome intrinsically low probabilities.

Again, take the example of your friend winning the lottery. This event has low intrinsic

probability in the sense that it seems highly unlikely that your friend will win. This low probability persists even if your friend buys tickets weekly. Nonetheless, if your friend does indeed win, simple, good evidence suffices to show this occurred. This good evidence can take many forms:

- Your friend calls you telling you he won and wants to celebrate.
- He posts his winning ticket on Facebook.
- Another trustworthy friend calls you to relay the information.

Although none of these establishes the event with strict certainty, they all serve as evidence that your friend won the lottery. Yet, who adduced any evidence out of the ordinary here? It seems that mundane, good evidence suffices to show it's reasonable to believe that an event with intrinsically low probability occurred.

2. Extraordinary evidence is evidence that meets an extremely high bar of probability.

On this view, extraordinary evidence establishes an event with, say, 99-plus-percent certainty, or close to it, such that no rational person could ever doubt it. So the skeptic claims. But we can challenge this.

First, observe that theses in other areas often seem to lack this extraordinary evidence. Consider three examples: 1) Caesar crossed the Rubicon. 2) The minimum wage is a good idea. 3) It is ethical to murder two innocent people to save a hundred innocent people.

These stock examples from history, public policy, and ethics underscore the point that an atheist will be hard-pressed to find "extraordinary evidence" of the type he defined in *any* domain. Sure, he may encounter some good arguments and strong evidence, but there will always be experts who disagree. He will hardly find the 99-plus-percent certainty he pursues.

We can ask the atheist, **"Is it irrational to believe that Caesar crossed the Rubicon, that the minimum wage is a good idea, or that it's unethical to murder two innocent people to save a hundred? If not, why not? Especially since these claims fail to meet your standards of extraordinary evidence."**

The atheist has a couple of options here:

a) Lower the bar of what counts as extraordinary evidence to a more reasonable level.

b) Reply that none of those examples from history or ethics constitute *extraordinary* claims, so they don't need extraordinary evidence.

If a) is chosen, then the conversation can resume along the lines that *good* evidence suffices to establish the rationality of a belief (even if such evidence is rather ordinary).

More likely, though, the atheist will argue b), maybe adding a point:

"The difference is that whether Caesar crossed the Rubicon has no impact on my life. I'm never going to be in those ethical dilemmas. Those answers make no difference. If Caesar were saying I had to renounce myself and follow him, that would be a much different story. So yes, extraordinary claims require extraordinary evidence and you should just admit that you don't have any."

At this point, we should note the change in terms the skeptic brought into the conversation. Now, it seems that "extraordinary events" are not rare or supernatural events, but rather "rare or supernatural events that dramatically impact our life choices." We can now proceed with this new addition to the terminology. Of course, if the atheist doesn't ever make this point, we do not need to answer it; I raise it because it's a fairly common response.

Principle 2: Very high bars of evidence for extraordinary claims will prove too much.

Note where we are in the discussion. The skeptic says that extraordinary claims that may dramatically impact life must meet a very high bar of evidence. I suggest asking the following question:

"Why do *extraordinary* claims need to meet this special high bar, yet *ordinary* claims do not?" Why is an especially high bar needed for believing in the resurrection of Jesus that is not required for the answers to public policy questions, ethical dilemmas, or trials by jury? Why exactly are extraordinary claims treated in such a special way? Why is this not special pleading? Listen carefully to the answer.

First, he simply points to the rarity or unexpected nature of *extraordinary* claims, we have already answered that.

Second, he might reiterate his point about the supernatural. "Supernatural events are unfathomable and wildly unbelievable in themselves," says the skeptic. He does not believe in supernatural events, so any such fanciful claims must meet a tremendously high bar of evidence. Here, atheism is presupposed. After that sort of answer, let the discussion turn to God's existence. If God exists, then he could work a miracle, and thus it could be reasonable to believe in a supernatural event.

Third, your conversation partner may argue that the *importance* of a claim renders it in need of extraordinary evidence. In other words, if something makes a big difference in a person's life, extraordinary evidence is required. But this cannot be right, since public policy questions and ethical decisions (for example) can make a big difference in someone's life, yet the skeptic likely does not require extraordinary evidence to take positions on them.

In response, you might ask, **"I'm curious, are you pro-choice or pro-life? Or do you take neither position?"** If he has a position on abortion, you might ask, **"What extraordinary evidence do you have in favor of that view? After all, it could make a big difference in the lives of many women and unborn humans, depending on how people answer."** It seems inconsistent and special pleading to apply the "extraordinary evidence" requirement to supernatural events and not to *all* important matters.

Frequently, this slogan reveals a prior commitment to naturalism. In turn, that leads us back to chapter one and the importance of fundamental worldview commitments. Edward Feser sums up the related issues in a blog post discussing Anthony Flew's assessment of David Hume's critique of miracle claims:

In any event, it is only if we presuppose naturalism that Hume's argument could have the completely general force against miracle claims that Flew thinks it has. If we have independent philosophical reason to think that naturalism is false, then that force is undermined and we have to consider the evidence for various miracle claims on a case-by-case basis rather than dismissing them wholesale the way Hume wanted to do.[39]

Additionally, do not take the discussion in this chapter as implying that the evidence for classical theism or the Catholic Christian worldview fails to meet even a high bar. After all, we have high-quality evidence for the Resurrection through the testimony of many witnesses, the rapid spread of the Faith and the widely attested miracles of the apostles and later saints, and the willingness of the martyrs to die for their beliefs, to name a few things. I do not downplay such evidence. My point here is that the skeptic has no good reason, other than his atheism, to set an especially high bar of evidence for religious claims.

Instead, we should look for *good reasons* and *good evidence* for the things that we believe. Good reasons and evidence suffice to show the rationality of belief in a claim, and if God exists, that can be the case even if a claim is wildly out of the ordinary.

COMING FULL CIRCLE

Since the arguments of this section have gotten a little complex, let's return to the skeptic's claim about a fire-breathing dragon and explain why it differs from the idea of a Catholic miracle.

If an "extraordinary claim" is a rare or supernatural event, then your friend having a fire-breathing dragon in his garage fits that definition. At first, you might think he's joking, and if you had no additional information, you would be justified in your skepticism. But suppose instead you asked him more about the dragon. You started looking for clues. You asked if anyone else had seen it. You examined how serious your friend defended his claim. In all probability, this investigation would reveal that there never really was a dragon in the garage.

However, the miracles that Christians believe in are not like the dragon case, for two reasons. First, because we believe that God performs them for a reason; they are connected with his revelation, not sporadic magic tricks. Second, they are backed up by credible witnesses and early testimony. Anthony Flew, at one time a very famous atheist who later adopted theism, said, "The evidence for the resurrection is better than for claimed miracles in any other religion. It's outstandingly different in quality and quantity."[40]

Christians don't believe *any* old miracle claim. Miracles can be investigated according to various criteria. But they cannot be ruled out *a priori* based on a slogan like, "Extraordinary claims require extraordinary evidence." If God exists, he can work a miracle, and we should investigate credible miracle claims to see what they reveal.

Questions to Ask

- "Could it be true that extraordinary claims require extraordinary evidence *and* that God exists?"
- "Would you agree that if God exists, then he could work a miracle?"
- "What do you mean by extraordinary claims?"
- "What do you mean by extraordinary evidence?"

- "Is it irrational to believe Caesar crossed the Rubicon? Or that raising the minimum wage is a bad idea? Or that it's unethical to murder two innocent people to save a hundred? If not, why not? Especially since these claims fail to meet your standards of *extraordinary* evidence."

- "Why do *extraordinary* claims need to meet this special high bar, yet *ordinary* claims do not?"

Middlegame Principles

- The slogan must be clearly defined before it can be assessed or employed.

- Very high bars of evidence for extraordinary claims will prove too much.

Recommendations for Further Study

- Read the article "Do Extraordinary Claims Require Extraordinary Evidence?" by Matt Nelson: https://www.reasonablecatholic.com/do-extraordinary-claims-require-extraordinary-evidence/.

- Watch this interview with Tim McGrew for a refutation of the slogan using sophisticated probabilistic analysis: https://www.youtube.com/watch?v=dOSuFkqrWsc.

- Read *Reasonable Faith: Christian Truth and Apologetics* by William Lane Craig (Wheaton, IL: Crossway, 2008).[41] This includes a historical defense of the Resurrection.

5

"All 'evidence' for God is based on God-of-the-gaps reasoning."

Perhaps it was once reasonable to believe in God, an atheist might say. But that was long before the scientific method. People used to believe in God because they didn't know what stars and planets were. They didn't understand what caused lightning, thunder, or earthquakes. So they attributed such events to various deities. From ancient times to now, however, science has slowly plugged in the *gaps* where we used to fit God. We no longer need to imagine gods to fill in those gaps in our understanding.

Notice the strong wording in this slogan. The proponent does not say *some* evidence falls into this category of God-of-the-gaps, but *all* of it. Let's consider how to respond.

OPENING RESPONSES

First, recognize that this skeptic makes a strong claim. He said "all" evidence for God is God-of-the-gaps. This implies that he has examined multiple evidences for God and judged them all to be of this kind. On this charge, I want to hear him out. So let's ask a question:

"How did you come to that conclusion?" Or if you want to be more specific, **"What is some of the evidence you have examined and what was wrong with it?"**

This provides the atheist space to back up the strong claim. It also provides you a chance to find some common ground. After all, some arguments for God that have been put forth are indeed God-of-the-gaps-type arguments. So you might agree on that point. But then you can ask another question, **"If *some* evidence is bad, does that mean *all* evidence is bad?"**

Of course, the answer is no. But the skeptic may insist, "No, but I've never seen any evidence that wasn't God-of-the-gaps." That provides you an opportunity to present some arguments. But before that, you may need to clarify one more thing.

Ask, **"What do you mean, exactly, by a God-of-the-gaps argument?"** Explain that you do not think all arguments for God commit this fallacy, and that some evidence is good. At some point, you should present some evidence and explain why you are not committing the fallacy. Later in this work, I summarize four arguments for God, and I provide a whole list of arguments and evidence for God's existence in appendix A. Here in this chapter, I'll use one example. But before that, do not forget to listen carefully to the answer to the question, **"What do you mean, exactly, by a God-of-the-gaps argument?"**

In all likelihood, the person has the following idea in mind: whenever someone sees some phenomenon he does not understand or cannot fully explain, instead of being honest and saying, "I don't know," he simply says, "God did it." By plugging in a gap with God, he demonstrates a refusal to admit his own ignorance. That's God-of-the-gaps reasoning.

In the middlegame section, I show that *some* reasoning does not commit the God-of-the-gaps blunder. But while setting the stage for this, I might ask one more question: **"I get that you have an issue with poorly thought-out God-of-the-gaps reasoning. But isn't it possible that God is the best explanation of some particular phenomenon?"** Of course, mere possibility does not prove the point, but it might get the skeptic thinking that at least some things might indeed be best explained by God. If someone is committed to dismissing all evidence as God-of-the-gaps, then he might miss out on a really good argument for God's existence.

Another question that might set the stage: **"Isn't it possible that God gave us some really good philosophical reasons to think he exists?"** Again, possibility does not show much. But it may serve to place a pebble in the shoe of skeptic who wants to rule out all evidence in advance.

MIDDLEGAME RESPONSES

Let's examine an argument for God, as well as some ways philosophers have addressed the "gap" problem.

Consider the Kalam cosmological argument:

Premise 1: Everything that begins to exist has a cause.

Premise 2: The universe began to exist.

Conclusion: Therefore, the universe has a cause.

The first premise has intuitive, philosophical support from the idea that *something cannot come from nothing.* Moreover, the negation of the premise is palpably false based on experience. We never see things popping into existence out of nothing. If things can come into existence out of nothing, then why don't we see this? As William Lane Craig says, "What's to stop bicycles or Beethoven from springing into existence out of nothing?"

Next, turn to the second premise: "The universe began to exist." Current scientific evidence strongly points toward this conclusion. In 2012, cosmologist Alexander Vilenkin reported, "All of the evidence we have says that the universe had a beginning." In an online article, Vilenkin writes, "The answer to the question, 'Did the universe have a beginning?' is, 'It probably did.' We have no viable models of an eternal universe. The BGV theorem gives us reason to believe that such models simply cannot be constructed."[42]

So, with strong evidence for both premises of the argument, we reach the conclusion that the universe has a cause. Now, before launching into that defense, I recommend asking your interlocutor, **"Have you ever considered the Kalam argument for God? What do you think of it?"**

If he has not considered it in any detail, you can lay it out in the way I've done here. But here's the key: the core syllogism represents what philosophers call "stage one" of arguments for God.

The Kalam cosmological argument is "stage one" of the argument because "stage two" follows next. If the argument stopped after "stage one" and you said, "See, God caused the beginning of the universe," that indeed would smack of God-of-the-gaps reasoning. However, philosophers of religions have adopted this "stage one" and "stage two" terminology to show *why* they are not merely plugging God into the gaps. Instead, they use further argument and explanation to defend truths about the reality arrived at in "stage one."

Throughout his book *Five Proofs of the Existence of God*, Edward Feser employs this method.[43] For each of the five proofs, he gives "stage one," which argues for some unknown reality responsible for various facts about our world. Then in "stage two" he shows why this unknown reality points to the existence of God.

Joshua Rasmussen follows a similar path in *How Reason Can Lead to God*. First, he shows there must be some *necessary foundation* to all reality (stage one). But the rest of the book is spent shining the light of reason on that foundation to see what it's like (stage two). Introduce this stage one/ stage two distinction to show your dialogue partner how philosophers deal with the "gap" concern.

Let's return to the Kalam cosmological argument. How might we move into stage two? William Lane Craig says that one can do a conceptual analysis of the cause to find out more of what it must be like. Since the cause brings it about that all space, time, matter, and energy exist (i.e., that the universe begins to exist), the cause cannot be a part of space, time, and matter. It must be *independent* of the material realm.

Thus, the cause of the universe is spaceless, timeless, and immaterial. Also, the cause of the universe is beyond our experience, or as we might say, it is *transcendent*.

Next, consider that the cause must have the *power* to bring about the effect of the universe existing (otherwise, how could it be labeled a cause?). This power could not be given to the cause at some *time*, since the cause is *timeless*. Therefore, the cause of the universe has a sort of *eternal power* to bring about the grand universe of our experience.[44]

Now, the skeptic may ask, "Yes, but why can't that cause just be some force or another dimension? Why does it have to be God? You see, you're still just filling in the gaps!" Notice, though, that at this point we are indeed starting to fill in the gaps. In other words, we now have good reason to believe in a spaceless, timeless, immaterial, transcendent, eternally powerful cause of the universe.

Return to the skeptic's question about a force or another dimension. In a way, we can agree that this cause has force (or power) and is something like another dimension in the sense of its being transcendent. But should we use the word "God"? For that, we want to show that this "cause" is not a mere *it*, but that it is in some sense *personal*, that we can relate to this cause in some way that people do not relate to forces or dimensions. Again, the Kalam proponent does not stop, throw up his hands, and say "Oh well, at this step we just say it's God!" Not at all. More stage two arguments are forthcoming.

Craig has defended several reasons for thinking the cause is *personal*. Here's one: consider the plausible candidates for being an immaterial cause. There are not many we can conceive of. There are 1) abstract objects and 2) unembodied minds. Yet, since abstract objects (like laws, numbers, etc.) do not cause anything, we must strike them from the list of candidates. Thus, we are left with one plausible candidate: the cause is an unembodied mind (or something mind-like).

I have found Craig's second reason even more persuasive. It goes like this. Why did the universe begin to exist rather than being always there? If all the antecedent conditions (forces, another dimension, etc.) were in place from all eternity, then why did the universe not emanate from them for all eternity? Why would it come to be at a moment in time rather than always existing? This conundrum cannot be solved by inanimate, eternal forces that cannot choose or decide to act.

However, it can be solved by that which has something analogous to *will* and can *choose* to bring the universe into being at a point in time. Having a will or choosing power is a fundamental aspect of personhood. Here we have another plausible reason to think the cause of the universe is personal.

Next we can ask: what is the best explanation of such a cause? One is that God exists. This conclusion of the theist seems eminently reasonable given the previous arguments. Another explanation is that the cause is something other than God. But what? What else fits that description? At the very least, we might ask our skeptical friend, **"Would it be reasonable to think that cause is God? If not, then why not?"**

If a conversation goes that far, it may need a rest. Allow your friend to have the last word and commit to revisiting the issue again in the future. After all, I have summed up the Kalam argument in a few paragraphs, though many books have been written on it.[45] The point in this exposition is to show that not all evidence is bad evidence. Not all evidence for God is God-of-the-gaps.

Finally, you might also point out that the "gap problem" is not new. St. Thomas Aquinas devotes many pages of his *Summa Theologiae* and *Summa Contra Gentiles* to arguments for various divine attributes (stage two). In particular, Aquinas argues for why that the unmoved mover, uncaused cause, etc., must be one, eternal, immutable, perfect, and so on. So natural theologians have known about this issue and taken it seriously for a long time.

Given all this, you might ask, **"Is it really plausible that all arguments for God are God-of-the gaps?"** If you have laid out the points above clearly, your friend might be able to answer no. Of course, that does not mean that all the arguments succeed. That consideration is where the discussion can turn next.

Questions to Ask

- "What is some of the evidence you have examined and what was wrong with it?"
- "If *some* evidence is bad, does that mean *all* evidence is bad?"
- "What do you mean, exactly, by God-of-the-gaps argument?"
- "Isn't it possible that God gave us some really good philosophical reasons to think he exists?"
- "Have you ever considered the Kalam argument for God? What do you think of it?"
- "Is it really plausible that *all* arguments for God are God-of-the gaps?"

Middlegame Principles

- Philosophers, ancient and modern, have deployed the stage one/stage two distinction to address this criticism. Present the Kalam cosmological argument as one example.

Recommendations for Further Study

- *Five Proofs of the Existence of God* by Edward Feser. This book uses the stage one/stage two distinction explicitly.
- *How Reason Can Lead to God* by Joshua Rasmussen. This book uses a stage one/stage two approach without explicit use of that language.

SERIOUS
SLOGANS

6

"If a loving God existed, his presence would be obvious."

This slogan has come to be known as the *problem of hidden-ness*. Along with the problem of evil, it is one of the two most popular objections to the existence of God. Although it is presented in a simple sentence as a slogan, philosophers have developed the objection and defended it at length—most famously, J.L. Schellenberg.[46] I think Christian apologists, particularly philosopher Michael Rea in *The Hiddenness of God*,[47] have answered Schellenberg's arguments decisively. In this chapter, I hope to give you some helpful material for handling the objection in conversation.

Consider this more sophisticated argument that develops the hiddenness slogan.[48]

1. God's perfect goodness and love imply that he would always be open to relationship.
2. If God is always open to relationship, then every finite person believes God exists unless he is somehow *resisting* such a belief.

3. If perfect-being monotheism is true, then there are no non-resistant nontheists.

4. There are non-resistant nontheists.

5. Perfect-being monotheism is false.

A typical amateur skeptic, though, may not present such a complex argument. He might instead just say something like this:

"Religious apologists keep trying to prove that God exists. Yet no one tries to prove that the Earth exists or that the sun exists. Surely the existence of God should be at least as manifest as that. Where is God hiding?"

With both hiddenness objections—the more sophisticated one and the man-on-the-street one—in mind, let's consider how we might respond.

OPENING RESPONSES

We need to listen to where the person is coming from who presents this argument. We might ask questions such as, **"That's an interesting point. Can I ask, did you ever once believe in God? What's your religious background?"** Let him explain. In all likelihood, at one time, he did believe in God but came to think he did not exist. Nonetheless, by listening closely you may detect important facts about what he has studied.

This slogan affords another opportunity to ask the Trent Horn question, **"What's the best evidence for God that you've heard and what do you think is wrong with it?"** After all, it's possible that this person got the sense that God was a made-up story and went asking people for evidence. Then, upon only hearing bad or subjective evidence, he went on to think there was no good evidence for God. At some point, he may have stumbled upon the point about divine hiddenness and thought, "Yeah, that seems right. If God really loved me, then he could easily just make himself more obvious."

Next, recognize that it's one thing merely to assert, "God is hidden!" but it's another thing to reach that as a conclusion after examining a good amount of evidence. If you ask our question from chapter one ("What's the best evidence you've heard...?"), the conversation can go back to the evidence for God, and you can refer to that earlier discussion for helpful replies.

Another question you can ask is, **"You say a loving God's presence would be much more obvious if he existed. How did you come to that conclusion?"**

We want to listen carefully for how this particular skeptic is thinking about God's hiddenness. For some people, this is a deeply personal issue, and a cold, calculated response could push them further away.

It's likely the person has two steps in mind that lead to that conclusion. First, looking around the world, to him it just seems that God isn't there. Second, he combines this "seeming" with an intuition about loving parents. When a parent loves a child, the parent wills the child's good in tangible ways and seeks to make the child's life a happy one.

It's also possible you've met someone who has perused atheist literature on the subject. This will be evident if you hear an assertion like this: "God's perfect goodness and perfect love imply he would always be open to a relationship." This sort of formulation has been made famous by Schellenberg, and it's precisely Schellenberg's argument that Michael Rea takes to task. But in a typical conversation, you don't have time to lay out Rea's comprehensive treatment.

So what can you say in response? For that, we turn to our middlegame responses.

MIDDLEGAME RESPONSES

I'll make six points to show why this slogan is not a strong argument against God. You might use two or three of these in a short conversation and refer to all of them in a lengthier discussion. A helpful acronym I have used for these six points is **NOMEAT**. For each point in the acronym, I provide a question you can ask to introduce the point. Here's the outline of all six points:

N—"God is **NOT** as hidden as some folks make it sound."

O—"Being more **OBVIOUS** doesn't necessitate more proper relationships."

M—"**MANY** goods are made possible through some degree of hiddenness."

E—"**EXPERIENCING** God does not require extraordinary visions or voices."

A—"**ADAM** and Eve's sin may be responsible for some hiddenness."

T—"**TRANSCENDENCE** demands having humble expectations concerning God."

First, God is not as hidden as some people think. To introduce this point, you can ask a question like this, **"When you look at the Mona Lisa, where is the painter hidden?"** This helps focus our idea. The painter is not visible *inside* the Mona Lisa, yet the painting *itself* points to a creator. Since God is not just another entity embedded inside the universe, we cannot expect to find him the way we grasp the existence of tables and chairs. Nonetheless, the universe cries out for a creator to explain why it exists. Although we may not have physical, tangible evidence of God, there are many good reasons to think God exists. St. Thomas Aquinas (1225-1274) taught we could know *that* God exists using reason alone. The Catholic Church formally supported this teaching at the First Vatican Council (1870-1871).

We can look at our universe and see *that* it exists, yet didn't have to (contingency argument), that it *began* to exist (Kalam argument), which calls for a cause, and that it exists in *just the right way* for the formation of carbon–based life (fine-tuning argument). So if you haven't asked it yet, this is a nice opportunity to take the discussion back to the evidence with the Trent Horn question, **"What's the best evidence for God that you've heard and what do you think is wrong with it?"**

Additionally, we might point out that most people throughout the centuries have believed in God. So, hiddenness has not prevented most people from believing.

Second, even if God were to make his existence more obvious, that might not lead more people into a loving relationship with him: "More **OBVIOUS** doesn't necessitate more proper relationships." The demons themselves believe that God exists but tremble in fear and hatred of him (James 2). Let's draw an analogy with eating healthy food.

Virtually all people know that they should eat healthy food and exercise to become healthier. But just because people know that this is the case, it does not follow that they will *act* upon that knowledge. In fact, many people, including me, often knowingly eat subpar food even when other, healthy options abound. Similarly, knowing that God exists may not lead to following him.

To introduce this point in conversation, you might ask, **"Do people ever freely choose what they know is bad for them?"** In all likelihood, your discussion partner will say yes, and then you can introduce the food illustration.

One can augment the force of this point by recognizing that many people are resistant to various Christian beliefs. Consider how many people resist Christian teachings regarding homosexuality, marriage, abortion, and euthanasia. Consequently, this resistance can create a psychological barrier that prevents people from experiencing God.

Exercise prudence when using this point in conversation, as it may come off as judgmental. But the truth is that some people are content to ignore God, to distract themselves, or to resist in small, subconscious ways God's invitation for relationship. Now, some skeptics might claim that they are non-resistant to truths of faith, but are open to seeing and reflecting on the evidence.

That's all well and good. When speaking with such skeptics, find out what evidence and arguments they have studied, and what holds them back. I might ask, **"I'm curious, what holds you back from trusting in God?"** or **"In your view, what are some good reasons not to trust in God?"**

However, just because an atheist *claims* to be non-resistant, that does not mean he actually is. Someone's inner truth can dodge detection even from his own introspection. Rea comments:

> Just think of what it would take to have good evidence—evidence sufficient to produce warranted belief—for the conclusion that someone's failure to believe

in God is *non-resistant* (never mind inculpable). Among other things, you would have to be able to acquire good evidence for the conclusion that resistance to belief in God, bias against relationship with God, and the like, have in no way colored her attention to assessment of the available evidence for God's existence. We have such limited access to the minds of others that it's hard to even imagine how one might acquire good evidence for such claims. Even if the person has never entertained the concept of God, she might, for all you could tell, have self-induced, even self-deceptive, biases against a relationship with a deity—*any* deity. For all you could tell, such biases might also color her attention to and assessment of such evidence that would otherwise point her to the existence of God. So how could you ever be in a position to say whether someone's failure to embrace theism is wholly free from influence by such biases?[49]

So it's not clear that mere knowledge that God exists will lead more people to believe. In other words, God being more **OBVIOUS** doesn't necessitate more proper relationships.

Third, we note that "**MANY** goods are made possible through some degree of hiddenness." What goods can come from the fact that God allows a degree of hiddenness? As a first thought, it makes the project of reasoning to God's existence an exciting and worthwhile endeavor. When a person learns mathematics, it requires little engagement to merely look up answers in the back of the math book. Working through challenging math problems step by step builds up our intellect and dignifies the discovery. Similarly, God wills that we seek and discover his existence in various ways that accord with our dignity as rational beings.

To raise this point, you might ask, **"Why shouldn't math students just look up and copy answers from the back of the book when doing homework?"** Explain that the dignity of discovery and learning in accord with our rational nature is lost when easy answers are provided.

Additionally, the true dignity of ethical behavior is preserved. If God were breathing down our necks, moral actions proceeding from genuine love would be hard to distinguish from those proceeding from fear. The self-sacrifice involved in genuine acts of courage and love may become less courageous and less loving. One question to motivate this consideration is, **"What do you think about someone who donates money to charity just to impress others?"**

Of course, the objection may arise that it's not fair for God to be hidden, since not everyone can reason to his existence. Additionally, being born in the wrong time or place, such as communist Russia, may prevent people from discovering the reality of God. How might we respond to this?

In the Christian tradition, our answer is that God provides sufficient grace for all to be saved. Everyone will be given enough light to come to a knowledge of him and attain salvation. In this life, that may not result in an explicit and well-articulated Catholic profession, but nonetheless, God's grace extends to the learned and unlearned alike. He provides enough light for those who seek to find him,[50]whereas those who refuse the light will stay in darkness.

So the goods of discovering the truth about God and of genuine, self-sacrificial love would be diminished in a world without hiddenness. To repeat: **MANY** goods are made possible through some degree of hiddenness. As such, it seems fitting that God be hidden to some extent from his creation.

Fourth, experiencing the divine does not require extraordinary religious experiences but is possible through mundane experiences with the right *cognitive lens*. How we *think* about our experiences can change the kind of experiences they are. What goes into this "right cognitive lens" will vary in religious traditions, but Michael Rea invites us to consider the following:

> Broadly speaking, there is consensus that the capacity to experience God can be developed through regular prayer, serious devotion to the cultivation of moral and spiritual virtue, and the development of various habits of mind that might reasonably be described as *seeking the presence of God, listening for God's voice, reaching out to God in love*, and the like.[51]

These divine encounters, as Rea calls them, need not involve visions, voices, or other supernatural manifestations that one might see in the movies. Why is that? Well, Rea points out that there is more to a perceptual experience than the perceptual content of the experience. Philosophers describe this by saying perceptual experiences are *cognitively penetrable*.

Consider hearing a noise in the middle of the night of a creaking house. You may form the belief, "It's an intruder," but you may also form the belief, "It's just the house settling." Your thought process is shaped, at least partially, by your experiences with creaking noises, intruders, and settling houses. This "cognitive lens" can give the experience richer content than *mere perception* of its phenomena. Another way of saying this is that experiences are *underdetermined* by perceptual content. From this underdetermination, it follows that *how we think* about our experiences becomes an essential component of those experiences. And if such thinking includes religious commitments, it can lead to divine encounters when one prays or reads the Bible. So one's personal cognitive lens brought to the table impacts the experience.

Consider how marriage can be impacted by our choices, habits, and cognitive lens. A husband can express love toward his wife by planning a date, selecting a preferred restaurant or activity, presenting flowers, and raising her favorite topics in conversation. Is he overjoyed when planning the date with all kinds of warm and fuzzy romantic feelings? Or does he find it to be a boring chore? Motivations, emotions, and feelings fluctuate over time. But the fact remains that the husband can *act* based on his marriage commitments that can lead to the deepening of the relationship. His choices, habits, and commitments all contribute to his cognitive lens, which in turn can lead to a more fully realized marriage bond.

So it is in our relationship with God. At different times in life we have more warm and fuzzy feelings (or more intense religious experiences) than at others. But despite how we *feel*, we can choose to orient our mind and habits toward God to grow the bond.

Now, some might think this is all crude subjectivism— that anybody with a certain "cognitive lens" could be said to have authentic experiences with unreal things (like the Easter Bunny or leprechauns). But that's a caricature. Our claim is that God is the type of reality that can be experienced by human beings through "a certain kind of skill," as Rea puts it, that is learned through practice and experience.[52] If the skeptic wants to claim that the Easter Bunny also can be experienced in that way, he's welcome to make his case. Meanwhile, it is both plausible and expected that a transcendent God would be experienced in this manner.

All of this undercuts the claim that religious experiences *require* perceptual content like paranormal visions and voices. With the right cognitive lens (which can be developed through personal and liturgical prayer, Scripture reading, moral improvement, etc.) people can experience God and relate to him in their ordinary living. Even if we never see a vision, we can still have religious experiences and grow in our relationship with God.

Here's a question to introduce this point: **"Have you ever heard of people having religious experiences? What typically comes to mind for you in that regard?"** Listen to the answer and instruct your interlocutor about how Christians have always held God can be found in the mundane. For a biblical example, consider the passage from 1 Kings and how the Lord speaks to Elijah:

> There he came to a cave and lodged in it. And behold, the word of the LORD came to him, and he said to him, "What are you doing here, Elijah?" He said, "I have been very jealous for the LORD, the God of hosts. For the people of Israel have forsaken your covenant, thrown down your altars, and killed your prophets with the sword, and I, even I only, am left, and they seek my life, to take it away." And he said, "Go out and stand on the mount before the LORD." And behold, the LORD passed by, and a great and strong wind tore the mountains and broke in pieces the rocks before the LORD, **but the LORD was not in the wind**. And after the wind an earthquake, **but the LORD was not in the earthquake**. And after the earthquake a fire, **but the LORD was not in the fire**. And after the fire the sound of a **low whisper**. And when Elijah heard it, he wrapped his face in his cloak and went out and stood at the entrance of the cave (1 Kgs. 19:9–13, ESV, emphasis mine).

In this passage, we can see that God need not be sought in powerful natural or supernatural events, but rather can be found in the quiet "low whisper" of daily prayer and religious life. You might even invite your conversation partner to seek

God and try talking to him. In the small moments of our daily lives, when we trust in God, pray, and seek, we can experience him in the everyday world.

Fifth, it's possible that "**ADAM** and Eve may be responsible for some degree of hiddenness." Christians hold that the fall of Adam and Eve was a real, historical event involving the disobedience of our first parents. Of course, Catholics may hold that the opening chapters of Genesis use figurative language.[53] But we don't need to take every detail of the story literally to conclude that there was a real, historical fall. And this fall led to grave consequences for the human race and the loss of preternatural privileges.

The author of Genesis portrays God walking with Adam and Eve in the garden in the cool of the day. Later, they are banished from the garden. In a common Catholic prayer, we declare ourselves to be "poor, banished children of Eve." We might apply this to the hiddenness problem as follows: God's walking with Adam and Eve represents a more intimate, immediate presence that was lost as a result of their sin. Now, we are born into a sinful world that lacks the intimate, immediate presence our first parents enjoyed. Though this does not completely solve the issue, it gives a plausible reason for why we would expect some degree of hiddenness.

It's true that the *Catechism* says, "After his fall, man was not abandoned by God" (410) it also says that, because of original sin, our human nature "is wounded in the natural powers proper to it, subject to ignorance, suffering and the dominion of death, and inclined to sin" (405). This means that our natural ability to know God has been damaged even though it wasn't completely destroyed.

You might introduce this point by asking, **"Have you considered that some degree of hiddenness might be the result of the fall of Adam and Eve?"**

Of course, the skeptic may quickly reply, "No, I haven't considered that because the story Adam and Eve is just a fairy tale!" At first this seems to nullify your question, but it's actually a subtle shift in the argumentation. Recall the dialectical context. The atheist presses a hiddenness objection in an attempt to support the view that God does not exist. In making the point about Adam and Eve, we show the atheist how, far from being a reason for rejecting the Christian worldview, some degree of hiddenness is actually *expected in* and *predicted by* it.

Sixth and finally, "**TRANSCENDENCE** demands having humble expectations concerning God."

As the necessary creator of all reality, the God of classical theism is radically different from us.[54] As such, we cannot judge God by the same standards as a mere human parent. We must have what Michael Rea calls a "humility about expectations" regarding how such a transcendent God will interact with his creatures. From *apparent* hiddenness, we cannot assume that God does not love us or that he does not exist, since God's radical otherness does not allow us to generate reliable predictions about his behavior.

We expect loving human parents to make their existence and love obvious and tangible to their children. But God is not a human being like we are. He did become human in the person of Jesus (and we have good evidence for this) and express love in a clear and tangible way when performing signs and miracles, as well as in offering his body for our salvation. But God, in his transcendence, is not a human being and thus cannot be bound by human expectations.

To introduce this point, we could start by asking, **"Is it possible that God has reasons for hiddenness that are beyond our comprehension?"**

God may have his own reasons or ways that are so far beyond us that we would not understand them even if we knew them better (see Isaiah 55:9, "my ways higher than your ways and my thoughts than your thoughts," and Romans 11:33, "how inscrutable are his ways?"). Yet, just because God's ways are beyond our comprehension does not mean he does not exist. It just means that skeptics cannot use human standards and expectations to disprove his existence.

That completes our six points that help defang the hiddenness slogan. Not every point will be relevant to every conversation. But they should serve as a well of information from which you can draw when a skeptic raises the problem of hiddenness. Over time, you may find even more effective ways of presenting these points in conversation.

Questions to Ask

- "That's an interesting point. Can I ask if you ever once believed in God? What's your religious background?"
- "How did you come to that conclusion?"
- "You say God is hidden, but what's the best evidence for God that you've researched and what do you think is wrong with it?"

Middlegame Principles

- Use the NOMEAT acronym to remember six points.
- N—God is NOT as hidden as some folks make it sound.
  - Ask, "When you look at the Mona Lisa, where is the painter hidden?"

- O—Being more OBVIOUS doesn't necessitate more proper relationships.
  - Ask, "Do people ever freely choose what they know is bad for them?"
  - Ask, "What holds you back from trusting in God?"
- M—MANY goods are made possible through some degree of hiddenness.
  - Ask, "Why shouldn't math students just look up and copy answers from the back of the book when doing homework?"
  - Ask, "What do you think about someone who donates money to charity just to impress others?"
- E—EXPERIENCING God does not require extraordinary visions or voices.
  - Ask, "Have you ever heard of people having religious experiences? What typically comes to mind for you in that regard?"
- A—ADAM and Eve may be responsible for some degree of hiddenness.
  - Ask, "Have you considered some degree of hiddenness might be the result of the fall of Adam and Eve?"
- T—TRANSCENDENCE demands being humble about expectations concerning God.
  - Ask, "Is it possible that God has reasons for hiddenness that are beyond our comprehension?"

Recommendations for Further Study

- Listen to the podcasts I did with Michael Rea, available for free here:

- www.classicaltheism.com/rea (part 1).
- www.classicaltheism.com/rea2 (part 2).
- Read Michael C. Rea's book *The Hiddenness of God*.

7

"Anyone who walks into a children's hospital knows that God doesn't exist."

This slogan refers to the problem of evil and suffering, which theologians have discussed for centuries. Dan Barker used it in a debate with Trent Horn.[55] In his opening statement, Barker says:

> You want to define God as a good being, right? Then all you have to do is walk into any children's hospital in the world and you know there is no God. You know that. Prayers are not answered. Those children are dying at the same tragic, sad rate as anyone else. Even with loving Protestant, Catholic, Jewish, Muslim families who care; they pray for God's protection. There's no difference. It makes no difference at all. If God was a loving being, there would be some difference. You would see atheists' children not surviving as well as those who are true believers. You would see something, but you don't. You don't see evidence at all.

A few moments later, the following exchange took place:

Dan Barker: Look at 9/11, all those people who prayed for God's protection. . . . If you knew 9/11 was going to happen and if you could've stopped it with no harm to yourself, if you could have done that, would you have? Would you have stopped 9/11?

Trent Horn: I'm willing to answer during cross-examination if you want to bring it up.

Dan Barker: You're not willing to say yes right now? Just say yes.

Trent Horn: I don't want to interrupt your time.

Dan Barker: No, say yes or no. You wouldn't have stopped it if you could have?

Trent Horn: Yes, I'd have a moral duty to stop it.

Dan Barker: Okay, so you're nicer than God [audience laughs]. . . . He let it happen. He could have stopped it. In fact, I would call that something of an accessory; he just stood there and let it happen. The God of the Bible is not only amoral but seems to be immoral.

The exchange looked very good for Barker, and undoubtedly many believers in the audience were challenged by it. Check out the entire debate to see Trent Horn's helpful responses. Here, we plan to respond to this difficult slogan: *Anyone who walks into a children's hospital knows there is no God.*

Of course, at the literal level, the slogan is patently false. Some people who walk into a children's hospital have a firm belief in God. But let's fill in the missing premises to strengthen the objection.

Anyone who walks into a children's hospital may see children suffering. A good God would not want children to suffer, and an all-powerful God could cure them. Indeed, a good, all-powerful God *would* cure them. Yet many die. Therefore, a good, all-powerful God does not exist.

The argument can also be found in the ancient Greek thinker Epicurus, who famously said:

> Is God willing to prevent evil, but not able? Then he is
> not omnipotent.
> Is he able, but not willing? Then he is malevolent.
> Is he both able and willing? Then whence cometh evil?
> Is he neither able nor willing? Then why call him God?

How can we go about answering Barker's arguments or the questions posed by Epicurus? Read on.

OPENING RESPONSES

First, find out precisely what the objector thinks. Avoid the mistake of launching into verbose explanations. He might say aggressively, **"Where was God when my sister died of cancer at the age of fifteen!"** Eloquent philosophizing in return may only make that worse. Pause and take a breath.

No matter how strong the person comes on, follow this two-pronged approach:

1. Pray for him silently. Something like this is good: "Jesus, have mercy on this son of yours and bring him into a deeper loving relationship with you."
2. Ask follow-up questions to frame the problem.

Evil and suffering present a problem to people in different ways. Is your conversation partner approaching it as an *intellectual* problem or a *pastoral* problem? This distinction should drive the discussion. Diplomatically, you should ask questions aimed at discerning whether he is approaching the problem as a philosophical puzzle or whether there are personal issues in the mix. (Or, if you know him well, you might just flat-out ask him.)

This distinction must be made because we handle those cases differently. Getting overly philosophical, interrogative, and accusative is exactly what Job's friends do wrong in the Bible's most famous book on suffering. Proper discernment at the outset will help us avoid this.

Grief over individual cases of evil marks the *emotional/pastoral* problem of evil. The person may reveal horrible encounters with suffering that left deep-seated feelings of sadness and betrayal. Any talk of God, especially philosophical talk, can seem distant, as the person may find it impossible to trust a God who would let these horrible things happen *to him* or the ones he loves. We will deal with Barker's points directly, but first let's consider the pastoral problem.

RESPONDING TO THE EMOTIONAL/ PASTORAL PROBLEM OF EVIL

If your discussion partner is going through something awful, how should you respond? There's no one right answer. Also, your particular response will depend on how well you know the person. A sibling conversation will differ from a conversation with a friend of a friend. What follows are three general points to keep in mind:

First, pray for the person. Offer some silent prayers and just sit there and be there for him, and don't try to over-analyze the situation. This is what Job's friends did right in the Bible. When they sat with Job and mourned with him, they acted rightly. However, when they opened their mouths and started analyzing the situation, they ceased to be helpful.

Second, if the person is a Christian, encourage him to take refuge in the love of Jesus Christ. Whereas other gods may appear distant or view mankind as a nuisance, Jesus loved us so much that he took on our human nature and endured horrendous sufferings for our redemption. Because he suffered in *real, tangible, terrible* ways (in his humanity), and because he knows our sufferings exhaustively (in his divinity), we can talk to him about it knowing that he comprehends all things. We can turn to him in prayer, knowing that he understands whatever we're going through. Encourage your dialogue partner to go to Jesus in prayer with all of his suffering and pain, and ask for his help.

Third, if the person is angry with God, you might let him know that the Bible contains examples of believers voicing complaints and protests. If he can't bring himself to pray to God in a pious manner, protest or complaint can be a legitimate temporary stage in his relationship to the almighty. One prominent biblical example is worth quoting at length:

> I am the man who has seen affliction under the rod of
> his wrath;
> he has driven and brought me into darkness without any
> light; surely against me he turns his hand again and
> again the whole day long.
>
> He has made my flesh and my skin waste away, and bro-
> ken my bones;

he has besieged and enveloped me with bitterness and
   tribulation;
he has made me dwell in darkness like the dead of long
   ago . . .

He has made my teeth grind on gravel and made me
   cower in ashes;
my soul is bereft of peace, I have forgotten what happiness is;
so I say, "Gone is my glory, and my expectation from
   the LORD" (Lam. 3:1-6, 16-18).

Realize that all those graphic protests and complaints are
inspired by God! Here, we find at least some warrant for afflicted people to relate to God by way of protest and complaint.[56] Nonetheless, that same author of Lamentations
maintains hope a few verses later:

But this I call to mind and therefore I have hope: The
   steadfast love of
the LORD never ceases, his mercies never come to an
   end;
they are new every morning; great is thy faithfulness.
"The LORD is my portion," says my soul, "therefore I
   will hope in him."

If nothing else, the person afflicted by suffering can cry
out to God through anger and protest. We can have hope
that such a relationship might eventually be healed by grace.
We ought to pray for grace to enter the lives of the people
who are suffering. Additionally, I suggest seeking the advice
of your parish priest or a spiritual director, as they will have
plenty of relevant pastoral experience.

Eventually, the person who went through suffering may seeks intellectual answers. Perhaps he finds himself *wanting* to believe in God again, but sees evil as an insuperable obstacle. That's where our intellectual preparation can be of service.

THE BAIT AND SWITCH

But before we turn there, I have one more note of caution: **people may swiftly switch back to the emotional problem as an attempt to cast doubt on intellectual answers.** What do I mean?

Your conversation partner might let on like he wants to examine the intellectual problem of evil. So, you offer some philosophical points for his consideration. Then, after hearing your explanation, he fires back, "Oh really? I bet you wouldn't dare say that to the family of a six-year-old who has cancer," or "Try telling that to the Jews in concentration camps during the Holocaust."

This type of retort can have strong emotional appeal. Your interlocutor might even phrase it as a question: "Are you seriously going to tell that to a six-year-old on her deathbed? That God has good reasons for giving her cancer when he could snap his fingers and cure it?"

Nonetheless, we must point out that our conversation partner has shifted the discussion back to an emotional problem of evil. In other words, they have renewed emphasis on what we would dare or dare not say to someone going through grave evil. But just because I would not necessarily say X, Y, and Z to a person going through grave suffering, it does not follow that X, Y, and Z are poor philosophical reasons. All that follows is that sometimes it may not be appropriate to discuss such things with someone who is suffering. So if this came up in conversation, I would point out,

"Hey, I realize that I may not say that to someone going through grave suffering, but it doesn't follow from that that these answers are bad answers. It just means sometimes we have to speak differently to people who are suffering."

After all, would an atheist dare say to that six-year-old that life is meaningless and death will be the end of her?

MIDDLEGAME RESPONSES

The intellectual problem of evil subdivides into the **logical problem of evil** and the **evidential problem of evil.** The logical problem of evil states that it is *impossible* for God and evil to coexist, because if he is all good and all-powerful he would not allow it. Proponents of the evidential problem hold that evil makes God's existence unlikely.[57] When handling the intellectual problem of evil, you should ask your discussion partner what type of argument he is offering: **"When you're looking at this philosophical puzzle, do you consider it *impossible* for a good God to exist given the evil in the world? Or do you think evil and suffering just make God's existence *unlikely*? In other words, you're offering them as evidence against God without arguing for an impossibility. Where do you stand on that?"**

We can formulate the logical problem of evil as an argument.

1. An all-powerful God could prevent all evil and suffering.

2. A perfectly good God *would* eliminate evil and suffering.

3. Yet, evil and suffering are manifestly present in our world.

4. Therefore, a perfectly good, all-powerful God does not exist.

This argument resonates with people at the level of common sense. When the atheist brings some particularly horrendous examples of evil to the table, he amplifies its force. Nonetheless, the logical problem of evil can be answered.

RESPONDING TO THE LOGICAL PROBLEM OF EVIL

To answer the logical version of the problem of evil, we want to show the argument given above is unsound. A sound argument has true premises and a conclusion that follows from those premises. So we either have to find a false premise, or show that the conclusion does not follow from the premises. It turns out one of the premises is indeed false. In our response, we should target premise 2.

1. A good God would eliminate evil and suffering as far as he can.

Many have called this premise into question for different reasons. Although it has superficial plausibility that a good God would eliminate evil and suffering, there are reasons to think that he would not. In fact, eliminating *all* evil and suffering would also require the elimination of many goods. So God may allow many evils in his creation as a way of bringing about various goods that could not otherwise be obtained. Let's consider some important examples of such goods.

First, it's a great good to make free creatures who can choose between good actions and evil ones. The great dignity that accompanies freedom of the will also leads to the possibility that people will abuse that freedom. Much of the evil in our world can be accounted for by such abuse.

Some critics reply that banishing free will would be a good thing! In support of their point, they argue a) free will is not worth the horrendous evil and suffering human beings cause, or b) the saints in heaven have freedom without the capacity to choose evil.

Regarding a), I first note that someone can reasonably hold that eliminating free will is not worth it, since it would lead to quite a different world where the best goods of freely chosen relationships fade away.

Regarding b), the critics are correct that the saints in heaven have freedom and will never choose evil. They might press, "Why not create a world with *only* heaven? Surely that would be better than this world full of evil and suffering." This question is dealt with differently among believers.[58] First, some responses call into question the idea that heaven could be the same with no prior earthly state. In other words, the joys and depths of loving relationships in heaven are *results of* a grace-filled life on Earth.

Second, we might point out that God may have reasons for creating a world like this prior to heaven, even if we do not grasp those reasons. In order for the logical problem of evil to prevail, the skeptic would have to show there cannot possibly be any good reasons for a world like ours. That is a heavy burden of proof, which is why many skeptics opt for a different version of the problem of evil (more on that soon).

Third, we should make the following point. **There are some goods that could not possibly come about in a world without evil.** These include courage, compassion, forgiveness, and self-sacrifice *in the face of* terrible evils. This explains why the critic is wrong who asserts that God should have just made a heaven-only world. It's true that in heaven there are free creatures who never go wrong, but if there were only heaven, then these goods would never be realized. Of course, an atheist might say, "But I'm fine with that! I don't want those goods," but that simply reduces the issue to the critic's preference.

But the critic's claim is actually much bolder than it seems. If he maintains that God should have created a heaven-only world, his position amounts to saying that God must never, under strict obligation, create a world with any of the particular goods (such as courage, compassion, forgiveness, etc.) that can follow evils. And if that's where the critic wants to hold ground, his objection reduces to an opinion we need not share. After all, if God wants to create a world with a multitude of goods, such as the ones mentioned, that is his prerogative.

At this point, the atheist may press us to discuss evils that have nothing to do with human actions, such as tsunamis, tornadoes, and diseases. How do we explain those sorts of evils? I recommend remembering the following Christian idea.

The fall of Adam and Eve explains why we live in a world of cosmic chaos, natural disasters, and disease. God created the world in a state of temporary harmony and perfection for our first parents, but when they sinned, they plunged our world into darkness, and human mortality entered into it.

In the Gospel of John, Jesus even speaks of evil, as personified by Satan, as "the ruler of this world" (John 12:32). And in Genesis 3, the consequences of Adam and Eve's actions are described with vivid imagery.

At that point in the conversation, the skeptic must choose between two options: 1) express disbelief in the fall of Adam and Eve,[59] or 2) grant the possibility of the fall and modify his objection to take that fact into account. The first option is not promising, since it's not going to be possible for the skeptic to show there were *not* two human beings who freely separated themselves from God at the dawn of time. So that leaves the second option.

Someone might grant the possibility of the fall of Adam and Eve and still push back that the punishment is too severe and unfair! Why should we, the sons and daughters of those parents, have to suffer such a horrible consequence when we did not commit the sin? Shouldn't we be created in the garden with our own choice? We can respond in two ways. First, God does provide each human being with the grace sufficient to be saved. So even if we are not given the bliss of the garden, we are given the choice of spending eternity with God. Thus, the consequences are not unfair in an ultimate sense.

Second, the consequences correspond to the gravity of the sin of separating from God. In this way they serve to warn us what life is like apart from God. The evils of disease and natural disasters show that without the special protection of God, as provided in the garden, life can be chaotic, tumultuous, and terribly painful. By capturing the gravity of separation from God, a fallen world with natural evils reminds us to turn to God for salvation. Of course, the critic may not like the result, but the cosmic chaos and natural disasters we experience can be traced back to the sinful choice of Adam and Eve in the garden.

RESPONDING TO THE EVIDENTIAL PROBLEM OF EVIL

Next, we consider the evidential problem of evil. This argument aims to show that it's *unlikely* or *improbable* that God exists given the evil and suffering in our world. Recall the principle from the introduction: **don't let people get away with vague, general criticisms**. In accord with that principle, ask, "Can you spell out the argument so I know what you have in mind?" Some may have the following formulation in mind:

> Premise 1: If pointless (or gratuitous) evils exist, then God does not exist.
>
> Premise 2: Pointless (or gratuitous) evils probably do exist.
>
> Conclusion: Therefore, God probably does not exist.

Note that this does not attempt to demonstrate a formal contradiction in holding to the existence of God and the existence of evil. Rather, the objector asserts it's merely unlikely that God exists. First, we might ask for further clarification: **"What do you mean by a 'pointless' or 'gratuitous' evil?"** Commonly, skeptics adduce the evils of Nazi Germany or kidnappers who rape and torture their victims.

These examples can appear overwhelming. Also, for someone dealing with the emotional/pastoral problem of evil, they can certainly seem to point to the non-existence of God. But we assume at this point in the discussion you are approaching the problem as an intellectual difficulty.

So what does the skeptic mean by "pointless" or "gratuitous" evil? Here are a couple of definitions he might supply:

- *Definition 1*: Evil and suffering that is of such a hideousness or magnitude that there can be no purpose or reason for its existence.

- *Definition 2*: A state of affairs that is not logically necessary to the attainment of a greater good or to the prevention of an evil at least as bad.

Here are a few points as to why the argument does not succeed in showing it's likely that atheism is true:

First, we cannot see all the picture of reality and how everything fits together over the course of human history. In other words, because we experience only a tiny slice of all human experience, we are not in a position to make such grand probability judgments. The key question to ask is, **"How do you know pointless evils *probably* exist?"**

The answer will likely be a list of horrible evils (Holocaust, rapists, etc.) coupled with the claim that they just *seem* pointless. However, the probability inference at work here is faulty, since *if God exists,* then he very well may have good reasons for the evil that occurs. Timothy Keller makes the point this way: "Just because you can't see or imagine a good reason why God might allow something doesn't mean there can't be one."[60]

William Lane Craig calls attention to two concepts that drive home the point of our limitations.[61] First, the butterfly effect refers to the concept that small things in the present lead to enormous effects in the long run. To take a stock example: a butterfly flapping its wings might change the weather pattern on a battlefield, changing the outcome of a war and the course of human history for the next 300 years. Likewise, chaos theory, a branch of mathematics, posits that one small change in a complex system can ripple through time, leading to future effects of extraordinary magnitude.

Human beings cannot see the future. We cannot even see most of the present. We don't know how a mere dozen of our neighbors might impact the world. Assessing all the causal influences and effects of billions of people over the course of history is a hopeless endeavor.

Since we cannot even fully comprehend the present, and we are entirely ignorant of the future, we are in no position to render probability judgments about the *pointless* nature of evils. This does not prove there are no pointless evils, but it does demonstrate that we simply are in no position to judge if certain evils are pointless.

For example, suppose a house catches fire in the middle of the night, killing a newborn baby and her parents. To us, this appears a pointless evil. However, our limited perspective prevents us from assessing all the effects of this event. As Craig notes:

> The brutal murder of an innocent man or a child's dying of leukemia could produce a sort of ripple effect through history such that God's morally sufficient reason for permitting it might not emerge until centuries later and perhaps in another land. When you think of God's providence over the whole of history, I think you can see how hopeless it is for limited observers to speculate on the probability that God could have a morally sufficient reason for permitting a certain evil. We're just not in a good position to assess such probabilities.

Second, our total evidence matters when discussing the question of God's existence. Here's an example. Let's say Fred is on trial for the murder of his wife. He claims innocence, but a witness testifies that she saw Fred stab his wife three times. Based on this alone, it doesn't look good for Fred. However, suppose later in the trial it comes out that Fred's wife was only stabbed *once,* and that the shade was closed on the window through which the witness had allegedly seen the crime. Suddenly, with the introduction of this new evidence, it is no longer clear that

Fred is guilty. Similarly, with God's existence, we should not gaze intently at the most horrendous evils and nothing else. we must weigh these in conjunction with arguments for God's existence as well as theistic explanations for evil.

As a second example, consider the theory of evolution, which holds that, over time, random genetic mutation and natural selection led to the emergence of a wide variety of life forms. Although the theory is widely accepted by biologists, many Christians question its veracity. Nevertheless, let us grant that the whole theory of evolution is true.

Next, consider the metamorphic process of caterpillars and butterflies. As discussed in several places,[62] the process exhibits such beauty and intricacy that it seems reasonable to judge there is an intelligent designer responsible for the creation of the butterfly. Moreover, evolutionary stories about natural selection and random mutations leading to such beauty and intricacy tend to sound implausible. So will the evolutionist relinquish his theory? Probably not.

Rather, biologists may argue that the total evidence supports the theory, even if certain things are difficult to explain. In a similar way, if we have good reasons to believe in God, then those same reasons can support our overall theory that God exists and simultaneously point against the probability of gratuitous evils. In other words, the evidential problem of evil does not exist in a vacuum. Seemingly pointless evils are not the only evidence on the table. So the theist can argue that the balance of evidence supports theism, even if various seemingly gratuitous evils serve as evidence against it.

If the person wishes to dismiss your point entirely, then to be consistent he cannot allow the evolutionist to argue in a similar way. In my experience, atheists want to protect arguments in favor of biological evolution. In so doing, they should also leave open our point: the question of seemingly gratuitous/pointless evils must be examined in light of our total evidence. And since we have good reasons to believe in God, we can say that seemingly pointless/gratuitous evils do not, all things considered, lead to atheism.

Third, mysterious evils are more likely if God exists than if God does not exist.[63] How might we develop this point? First, consider that idea of "if-then" testing. We can ask, *if* God exists, would we expect some horrendously mysterious evils? Second, we can ask, if God does *not* exist, would we expect some horrendously mysterious evils?

Suppose God exists and has created the entire universe according to a grand story that he is working out over time. Joshua Rasmussen develops this line of thought:

> I would expect the usual elements of a grand story, including scenes suited for heroes, and episodes of uncertainty. Moreover, I would expect co-authors of a real story. I would expect to find kingly characters who can help decide how things unfold. And, if things unfold poorly, I would expect the ultimate author to work bad things for good.
>
> Also, I would expect some of God's reasons to be above my current knowledge.[64]

So it is at least plausible that *if* God exists, there would be some likelihood of mysterious evils. Rasmussen sums this up by saying, "the likelihood of at least some mysterious evils if God exists is *not low*."[65] Contrast this with the probability of mysterious evils in a world where God does not exist. What's the likelihood that evil would exist in such a world? Well, evil would need to arise in a world that did not have a good, wise, and powerful foundation (i.e., God).[66]

Nonetheless, in order to have mysterious evil, we need the world to be set up just right to get conscious individuals who can detect right from wrong. Without conscious moral agents, there could be no one to experience the mysterious evils. Yet, a fine-tuned universe that can produce such individuals seems astronomically improbable, if not impossible, if God does not exist. I argue for this in appendix B when defending a fine-tuning argument. If that argument works, it allows this point regarding mysterious evils to succeed. Since the probability of mysterious evil is greater if God exists than if he does not, these mysterious evils do not constitute powerful evidence against theism.

Fourth, horrendous evil can be medicinal or spiritually motivating in crucial ways. Eleonore Stump puts forward the Bible story of Cain and Abel as she invites us to consider who is in more danger as Cain plots to kill Abel? In reality, Cain, the murderer, is in the worse position, since he risks cutting himself off from God for eternity. He can kill Abel, but Abel's existence does not end at death. Life consists of two unequal portions: a short, finite, earthly existence and an unending existence in the afterlife.

On the Catholic Christian worldview, our earthly existence is but a small blip in our lives. We all have an eternal destiny of final glory with God or permanent separation from him. But if that is the case, then by providing an arena full of horrendous suffering, God can remind people of their mortality and move them to repent and turn to him. As C.S. Lewis famously said, "God whispers to us in our pleasures, speaks in our conscience, but shouts in our pains: it is His megaphone to rouse a deaf world."[67]

My fifth point draws upon the work of the Dominican priest and philosopher Brian Davies. He explains that God's goodness need not be construed in moral terms. Here's why.

People are morally good when they act well with respect to various duties, obligations, and other moral imperatives. They live in a world where they have freedom to choose good actions or bad ones. They can improve or regress over the course of their lifetimes. They are beings in the world, living in a moral community where good and evil can be judged according to various ethical frameworks.

But, when we consider the God of classical theism,[68] we see that he does not fit the description of a moral agent. He is perfect and immutable in himself. He is not some cosmic Boy Scout who needs to get all the merit badges to be considered good. Since an immutable, necessary, perfect being must be radically different from us, we cannot generate expectations about what his goodness should and should not allow. Whatever God's goodness is, it should not be confused with the goodness of a human moral agent.

Although we are tempted to bring God's ways down to our ways, the *Catechism* reminds us that God is radically transcendent:

> Admittedly, in speaking about God like this, our language is using human modes of expression; nevertheless it really does attain to God himself, though unable to express him in his infinite simplicity. Likewise, we must recall that "between Creator and creature no similitude can be expressed without implying an even greater dissimilitude"; and that "concerning God, we cannot grasp what he is, but only what he is not, and how other beings stand in relation to him" (CCC 43).

That sets the stage for speaking about God's goodness in a different way. Fr. Davies argues that "God is good" can still be affirmed as a true statement in the following ways:

- He is perfect, and anything that is perfect should be considered good.[69]

- He is the cause of all creaturely goodness, which means that all goodness in creatures must exist in him in a pre-eminent way.[70]

- He is the most desirable being, and that toward which all things aim. To be good is to be in some way desirable, and so God is good in that sense.[71]

Notice, none of these ways of being good entail that God is *morally* good. By this, we do not mean that God is *morally bad* or even *morally indifferent*. Rather, we mean that God's goodness is not bound by the categories of creaturely moral agency; God cannot be thought of as a person living in the world and doing a good job or bad job of it. As the simple, immutable, and perfect creator, his goodness is radically different from that of human moral agents. It's not false to say, "God is good," but we should not deduce from this truth that God's goodness must be thought of as moral goodness.

So as far as the objector attempts to impugn God's moral character with his argument, the argument is a nonstarter. As Joshua Matthan Brown puts it, "What is really on the line when theologians defend various theodicies[72] (or skeptical theism, or whatever) to account for gratuitous evil is not the existence of God but, rather, the nature of God's goodness."[73] If God's goodness is unlike that of a human moral agent, we cannot condemn him (or deem him nonexistent) for permitting what we as human moral agents would not permit.

Karlo Broussard sums up a similar point this way:

God not only has no obligation to create a particular type of world, he has no obligation to create in the first place.

In fact, he has no obligation whatsoever. If he did, he would not be God. Obligation necessarily implies subjection to law . . . Furthermore, obligation to law implies the possibility of change . . . These aspects of obligation do not apply to God.[74]

Now, this still leaves open questions about how God is *causally related* to evil. On this score, Fr. Davies provides a detailed account in line with the teaching of St. Thomas Aquinas.[75] Entering that discussion goes beyond the scope of our chapter, but I recommend several resources at the end of the chapter for those interested in learning more.

A lot more could be said about the problem of evil, but we will stop here. We spent more time on this chapter as it is the most famous objection to God's existence, and it cannot be answered in the same pointed fashion in which it's often raised. However, using the tools and points from this chapter, you can situate the problem carefully and offer something more for your dialogue partner's consideration.

FULL CIRCLE WITH DAN BARKER

Recall the end of the exchange between Dan Barker and Trent Horn:

> **Dan Barker:** No, say yes or no. You wouldn't have stopped it if you could have?
>
> **Trent Horn:** Yes, I'd have a moral duty to stop it.
>
> **Dan Barker:** Ok, so you're nicer than God [audience laughs]. . . . He let it happen. He could have stopped [9/11]. In fact, I would call that something of an accessory;

he just stood there and let it happen. The God of the Bible is not only amoral but seems to be immoral.

Let's close this chapter with a brief response to Barker. His illustrations of 9/11 and the Holocaust have strong emotional appeal. We cannot doubt that. But if the aim is to put forth a philosophical argument against God's existence, more work must be shown. First, we should ask Mr. Barker, **"Are you putting forth a logical problem of evil? Are you saying it's impossible for God to exist given events like 9/11?"** Suppose that is what he intends. In that case, we can point out two major things.

First, God's creating and preserving men with the dignity and freedom to choose good or evil allows for the possibility of crimes as evil as the Holocaust. Yes, God could simply annihilate people who choose evil or zap their weapons out of existence, but doing so would mitigate their dignity as free moral beings.

Of course, the atheist can respond, "But I'd rather have that if it meant less evil and suffering!" But although that may be what he prefers, it does not follow that such a world is logically required. His logical problem, if it is to show that God and evil cannot possibly coexist, cannot rest on a mere preference.

Second, notice how Trent replied, "Yes, I'd have a moral duty to stop it." Human beings living in the world have ethical duties to others. Failing to prevent a gross injustice when we could have easily done so is wrong *for human beings*. Nonetheless, we may wonder, is that same analysis applicable *to God*? The answer given by Fr. Davies, and other classical theists, is no. God has no moral obligations because he is not a moral agent like human beings are and there is no law higher than himself to which he must submit. Rather, God is good, but his goodness is not like our goodness.

So although we may witness human moral failures and infer that the negligent person is not all good, we can't make a similar inference in the case of God. God is not a human moral agent with an obligation to prevent our free choices from bringing about calamity. If he chooses to step in on a case-by-case basis, such mercy is his prerogative. But that mercy is not owed to us. The God of classical theism has created us with the freedom to choose good or evil, and preventing the evil choices of men is not required to maintain his goodness.

Questions to Ask

- "I want to give your objection a fair hearing, so I'm curious: are you coming at this problem as an intellectual, philosophical puzzle? Or are you coming at it as someone who is going through something terrible in the moment?"
- Distinguish the logical and evidential problems of evil.
    - The logical problem of evil aims to show it's impossible for God and evil to coexist.
    - The evidential problem aims to show that evil (or particular evils) make God's existence unlikely.
    - Ask, "When you're looking at this philosophical puzzle, do you consider it *impossible* for a good God to exist given the evil in the world? Philosophers call that the logical problem of evil. Or do you think evil and suffering just make God's existence *unlikely*? In other words, you're offering them as evidence against God without arguing for an impossibility. Where do you stand on that?"

Middlegame Principles

- Offer a few ideas for answering the **logical problem of evil**:
  - It's a great good for there to be a world of free creatures who can choose between good actions and evil ones.
  - The fall of Adam and Eve explains why we live in a world of cosmic chaos, natural disasters, and disease.
  - Some goods could not possibly be manifested in a world without any evil.
  - So the existence of *some* evil is not a good reason to reject God's existence.
- Offer a few ideas for answering the **evidential problem of evil**:
  - We cannot see the whole picture of reality and how everything fits together over the course of human history. God can draw good out of evil, and we're not in a position to say good cannot come from particular evils.
  - Our total evidence matters when discussing the question of God's existence.
  - Mysterious evils are more likely if God exists than if God does not exist.
  - Horrendous evil can be medicinal or spiritually motivating.
  - God is not a human moral agent and his goodness is not moral goodness.
  - So the existence of seemingly gratuitous evil or mysterious evil is not a good reason to reject God's existence.

Recommendations for Further Study

- Read *Prepare the Way* by Karlo Broussard, in which he develops questions and tactics for answering the problem of evil.

- Read *The Reality of God and the Problem of Evil* by Fr. Brian Davies for an approach to the problem that incorporates Aquinas and others in the tradition of classical theism. Fr. Davies also wrote a shorter book that expounds many of the same points: *God and Evil in St. Thomas Aquinas*. For an introduction to his thoughts on the subject, you might consider the podcast dialogue I recorded with Karlo Broussard based on one of Fr. Davies's articles: www. classicaltheism.com/evildialogue.

8

"If God inspired only one religion, we wouldn't have so many different ones."

The primary meaning of this one goes like this: if God is truthful, loving, and clear, *why is there so much religious disagreement?* (It shares some similarities with the hiddenness objection—if God really existed, he would reveal himself clearly.) The best explanation to the diversity of revealed religions, it continues, is that no revealed religion is correct.

OPENING RESPONSES

First, as usual, you should start with questions. Ask, **"How did you come to that conclusion?"** and allow the person to explain his thought process.

Second, point out that this slogan does not really present a case for atheism, since it doesn't show that there is no God. At most, it shows that we have been wrong about divine revelation. Point this out and ask, **"Isn't it possible that**

God exists, but what he revealed to us has been misinterpreted or misappropriated?"

If he insists that it does prove God's non-existence, he has further explaining to do. Ask, **"How does it lead to that conclusion? Isn't it possible that God exists but simply did not reveal himself in texts or miracles?"** If your conversation partner does not grant this, the discussion likely will not be fruitful.

Nonetheless, since Catholic Christians believe in divine revelation from God, we ought to answer the objection in its strongest form. Here is an extended elaboration of the argument from atheist philosopher Ben Watkins. He writes:

> Our concept of a perfect being implies a concern for the religious content of our beliefs and the moral value of our characters and acts. But if we assume theism is true, then it seems as if God has inconsistently or inaccurately revealed what He wants us to believe and how He expects us to act. By contrast, if atheism is true, then there is no disembodied mind who cares about the content of our religious beliefs nor the moral worth of characters and acts. Widespread disagreement about the nature and significance of experiences which do not correspond to a shared objective reality is not surprising if atheism is true. I concluded facts about widespread religious disagreement count in favor of atheism and against theism.[76]

Let's start with a question similar to the one I asked above: **"Even if all you say is correct here, it wouldn't show that atheism is true, right? After all, couldn't God exist and not act in accord with your expectations?"**

Of course, the atheist may agree and say, "Perhaps, but it would disprove Christianity, since the Christian God is supposed to be all good, all-powerful, and all-knowing." Again, ask that the person clarify: **"How *precisely* does the argument count against Christianity? Can you spell it out?"**

Not only does this slogan not disprove Christianity—the argument is fully accounted for by Christianity. In particular, the Catholic worldview provides resources to account for religious disagreement without abandoning theism. Let's turn to those ideas.

MIDDLEGAME RESPONSES

In this section, we examine five points within the Catholic worldview to handle the challenge of religious disagreement:

1. **Multiple claims to truth do not imply that there is no truth.** We can see this throughout history, for example in the history of science. Over the centuries, people had all sorts of theories to account for natural phenomena, but that variety of views did not mean there was no correct view in any case.

   You can introduce this point with an analogy and a question: **"Does the existence of counterfeit money show there is no real money?"** Your discussion partner may answer "no" and then add something to press the objection further. That's a good thing, and it allows you to see more of what he has in mind. He may argue something like this: "Yes, but if God reveals only one religion, he should do so clearly so that there would not be any other ones. The fact that there are so many religions shows that God did not adequately reveal himself. So he probably doesn't exist." You can respond with further points enumerated below.

2. **Widespread religious disagreement may be due in part to a widespread religious impulse within a fallible human race.** Most human beings throughout history have believed in God in some sense. Since they believed in God, it's not surprising that they attempted to find God and draw conclusions about him on their own. Being fallible, these conclusions were prone to error. Add to this that human beings are not only fallible (prone to error) but also vicious (prone to doing evil), and we can see how some would falsely claim divine revelation for their own gain.

The objector might press that a good God should intervene to stop people from committing such hoaxes. This morphs the slogan into a form of the problem of evil, which we dealt with in the previous chapter.

3. **The fall of Adam and Eve, through which sin entered the world, is the root cause of our living in an imperfect world—complete with pain, suffering, disease, disasters, and yes, religious disagreement.** Nonetheless, God has a rescue plan, according to Christianity, and the created order is in a state of "journeying" toward perfection. As the *Catechism* states eloquently:

> Creation has its own goodness and proper perfection, but it did not spring forth complete from the hands of the Creator. the universe was created "in a state of journeying" (*in statu viae*) toward an ultimate perfection yet to be attained, to which God has destined it. We call "divine providence" the dispositions by which God guides his creation toward this perfection (CCC 302).

Religious disagreement in our world, then, can be explained by the choice of our first parents to turn away from God. It doesn't disprove God's existence or the truth of Christianity. And according to Christianity, it's temporary. In heaven there will be no more religious disagreement.

4. **According to the Catholic Church, God gives all men sufficient grace to be saved, but some freely choose to reject that grace.** I think the biggest concern behind this slogan is that some people won't get a fair shake in life. Objectors may worry that, according to Christianity, those born into other religious traditions or those born at the wrong time and place will automatically be damned. (We'll talk about this some more in chapter eighteen.)

Despite God's permitting religious disagreement, he provides enough light to all men, such that if they respond to his grace, they can find salvation. This does not imply that all religions are equally salvific or that there is a plurality of paths to God. Jesus says, "I am the way, and the truth, and the life, and no one comes to the Father except by me" (John 14:6). And the *Catechism* asserts, "All salvation comes from Christ the Head through the Church which is his Body" (CCC 846). But the Church also maintains that "in ways known to himself God can lead those who, through no fault of their own, are ignorant of the gospel, to that faith without which it is impossible to please him" (CCC 848).

So God gives to all men, even those born into different religions, the chance to be saved; and insofar as they are saved, they are saved through the grace of Jesus Christ and his Church.

5. **Willful and culpable ignorance also accounts for some measure of religious disagreement.** In *Five Proofs of the Existence of God,* Edward Feser writes, "Just as God allows us a very long leash with respect to errors in what we *do*—even to the extent of moral breakdown at the level of entire societies, genocide and other atrocities, and so forth—so too does he allow us a very long leash with respect to errors in what we *think.*"[77]

According to the Catholic tradition, God has revealed himself through his creation and in ways that can be known by the natural light of human reason. Suppose someone learns this and comes across some evidence for God. For example, suppose a friend buys him the book *How Reason Can Lead to God* by Joshua Rasmussen. If the person refuses even to look at the book and to consider any of the reasons to believe in God, then he *chooses* to remain ignorant about the topic.

Or suppose the person is offered evidence for the resurrection of Jesus or some other miracle but refuses to consider it or investigate it. Again, by his choice he remains ignorant of these motives for faith. So the "long leash" that Feser describes can include the free decisions of men who culpably refuse to examine the evidence honestly. To the extent that ignorance is culpable, only God knows for sure, but one cannot deny that willful ignorance accounts for some religious disagreement.

In the course of a conversation about religious disagreement, you must discern which points will be most helpful to your discussion partner. Nevertheless, for the reasons laid out above, this slogan does not favor atheism over Christianity.

Questions to Ask

- "This wouldn't mean that *atheism* is true, right? God could exist but we still might get his revelation wrong."
- "How does the argument count against Christianity? Can you spell it out?"

Middlegame Principles

- The existence of counterfeit money does not mean there is not true money.
- The widespread religious impulse among fallible, sinful humans leads to religious error and false revelations.
- The fall of Adam and Eve accounts for the imperfection of our world, and one of those imperfections is religious disagreement.
- God gives all men sufficient grace to be saved.
- Culpable ignorance accounts for some measure of religious disagreement.

Recommendations for Further Study

- Read chapter 13 of Josh Rasmussen's book *How Reason Can Lead to God*.
- Read the *Catechism of the Catholic Church*, paragraphs 830 to 848.

9

"The God of the Bible is an evil maniac who commits atrocities."

This slogan is very popular with atheists on the internet. They trot out various examples of difficult Bible passages and exclaim, "See! Even if God exists, he's clearly an evil maniac and no one should worship him!" They may call to mind the great flood or commands for the Israelites to conquer the Canaanites.

Citing many different examples, the atheist Dan Barker wrote a book titled *God: The Most Unpleasant Character in All Fiction*. That book title echoes the influential words of Richard Dawkins from his book *The God Delusion*:

> The God of the Old Testament is arguably the most unpleasant character in all fiction: jealous and proud of it; a petty, unjust, unforgiving control freak; a vindictive, bloodthirsty ethnic cleanser; a misogynistic, homophobic, racist, infanticidal, genocidal, filicidal, pestilential, megalomaniacal, sadomasochistic, capriciously malevolent bully.[78]

In order to prepare for this slogan, we will tackle specifics related to God commanding killings as well as the problem of slavery in the Bible.

OPENING RESPONSE

Check if the skeptic has done his homework. Remember the important principle: do not let him get away with vague accusations. Ask, **"What specifically do you have in mind?"** Maybe he will respond, "Are you serious? God kills everyone and orders people to rape people. It's disgusting!" Still, you must press the person for substance. Ask, **"Can you provide some more specifics? Where in the Bible does God do this?"** In fact, God does not order anyone to rape in the Bible.

Next, we can point out that Bible difficulties do not by themselves show that God does not exist. Ask, **"Even if there are issues with the Old Testament that we do not know how to handle, that wouldn't show that God doesn't exist, right?"** Perhaps your friend will grant the point, though he may insist such considerations would disprove Christianity. I don't think that's the case. To show why, simply respond, **"I don't think it would show Christianity is false, since Christians primarily rest their faith on Jesus. It's true that Christians believe the Bible is inspired, but at most these objections would require us to revise our view of inspiration. What do you think about this?"**

Of course, Christians should not shy away from affirming inspiration and inerrancy. The Church has taught this in many places. For example, in an important document from the Second Vatican Council, we read this:

In composing the sacred books, God chose men and while employed by him they made use of their powers and abilities, so that with him acting in them and through them, they, as true authors, consigned to writing everything and only those things which he wanted.

Therefore, since everything asserted by the inspired authors or sacred writers must be held to be asserted by the Holy Spirit, it follows that the books of Scripture must be acknowledged as teaching solidly, faithfully and without error that truth which God wanted put into sacred writings for the sake of salvation (*Dei Verbum* 11).

So we will want to offer a response that does not give anything away. Nevertheless, situating the objection with those initial questions is important, since Bible difficulties alone cannot show that atheism is true and Christianity is false. In the next section, we examine specific principles and ideas to keep in mind in a conversation in which someone claims, "The God of the Bible is an evil maniac."

MIDDLEGAME RESPONSES

Here we look at how to respond without giving up the Bible or a traditional doctrine of inspiration. Suppose the skeptic produces the example of the Flood or Israel's conquest of the Canaanites. It is true that the Bible reports God telling the Israelites to wipe out every man, woman, child, ox, and other animal in the land occupied by the Canaanites.[79] But what is not clear is that this therefore makes God an evil maniac. I see three main points we can make to show this.

First, as the author and creator of all life, God has unique authority over human beings such that he can give and take life as he sees fit. As the author of life, he has prerogatives and authority that we do not have. It would be morally wrong *for human beings* to run around killing innocent people in order to conquer lands or bring about justice. But it is not wrong *for God* to give and take human life as he sees fit. To highlight God's special authority, Karlo Broussard provides a helpful question to ask: **"Is it unreasonable for an ambulance driver to run a red light when we may not? Is it unreasonable for a principal to cancel classes for a day although a student or teacher can't?"**[80] Of course, both of these cases are reasonable. How much more reasonable is it then for God, the creator, to act with an unmatched authority?

We can take this line of thought further. This might be a hard truth to swallow, but God is not in debt to his creatures and he does not owe any of us a long life. Whether our time on Earth is brief or drawn out, God commits no injustice when he permits or commands it to come to an end. So if God commands the Israelites to wipe out the Canaanites, then Israel's army can do this on God's authority, acting as instruments of divine commands. Nonetheless, in the absence of such special divine commands, it would be unjust for Israel's army to act in the way described.

An objection usually pops up at this point. Some worry that Christians will just start claiming randomly that God told them to kill people. The atheist might even say, "Are you saying that if some guy says God told him to kill a bunch of innocent people he can just go do it? That's madness!"

However, as Catholics we have a clear answer to this. The Church has taught that public revelation ceased with the death of the last apostle. So we don't need to worry about God inspiring people to wipe out other nations by divine command. That occurred at a certain time and place while revelation was unfolding, and God spoke specifically to Israel. Those conditions no longer hold today, since revelation has ceased. Thus, we can rightly resist people who claim to hear voices from God telling them to murder or disobey his commandments.

Second, point out that God's judgment will be *perfect* and there will be no mistakes. Some may worry that innocent people swept away in the calamity God commands could accidentally end up in hell. But that simply isn't possible on Christian premises. If people are united to God upon their death, then God will welcome them into the heavenly banquet. If people have willfully separated themselves from God through mortal sin, then God will not welcome them into his kingdom after death. So God's perfect judgment will not result in any eternal injustices.

If some people have not committed any mortal sins because they were too young (infants, say), then they cannot be condemned to eternal separation from God. They either attain heaven through God's mercy or, as is the opinion of some in the Catholic tradition, a natural happiness, the limbo of unbaptized children. But the main point stands: God's judgment will be perfect and there will be no mistakes.

Third, some have argued that the commands to the Israelites to wipe out everyone and everything ought not be taken literally. Paul Copan develops this idea in his excellent book *Is God a Moral Monster? Making Sense of the Old Testament God*. Trent Horn devotes considerable space to this line of thought in his book *Hard Sayings*.

Bringing forth examples from the ancient Near East, Copan and others argue that some of the commands are consistent with "warfare rhetoric" of the day. There's certainly some evidence in support of this reading, and it may mitigate the revulsion some skeptics experience upon reading warfare passages. Nonetheless, as argued above, even if the commands are literal, it does not follow that the God of the Bible is an evil maniac.

Questions to Ask

- When someone asserts, "God is an evil maniac," ask that he clarify what that means.
- "Can you provide some more specifics? Where in the Bible does God do this?"
- "Even if there are issues with the Old Testament that we do not know how to handle, that wouldn't show that God doesn't exist, right?"
- "I don't think it would show Christianity is false, since Christians primarily rest their faith on Jesus. It's true Christians believe the Bible as a whole is inspired, but at most these objections would seem to require us to revise our view of inspiration or inerrancy. What do you think about this?"

Middlegame Principles

- The God of classical theism is not a moral agent like human beings are but is the necessary creator of the universe who has authority to give and take life as he sees fit.
- Ask, "Is it unreasonable for an ambulance driver to run a red light when we may not? Is it unreasonable for a principal to cancel classes for a day although a student or teacher can't?"
- God's judgment will be perfect.
- Some have argued that the commands to wipe out the Canaanites are not literal.

Recommendations for Further Study

- Read the book *Hard Sayings* by Trent Horn.
- Read the book *Is God a Moral Monster?* by Paul Copan.

SLOGANS ABOUT FAITH & EVIDENCE

10

"It's irrational to believe things without evidence or to pretend to know things you don't really know."

This slogan targets a particular understanding of faith. According to the sloganeer, *faith* consists of "belief without evidence" or "pretending to know." Some atheists will go so far to say that faith is "believing what you know ain't so." Faith should be cast off because it is a form of glorified irrationality. Instead of faith, we should prefer facts and evidence.

In a YouTube video, Neil De Grasse Tyson makes a point that exemplifies the slogan:

> I have no problems if as we prove the origins of things we bump up into the bearded man. If that shows up, we're good to go. Okay. Not a problem. There's just no evidence of it. And this is why religions are called *faiths*, collectively: Because you believe something in the absence of evidence. That's what it is. That's why it's called faith.

Otherwise we would call all religions evidence! But we don't for exactly that reason.[81]

How should we respond to this?

OUR RESPONSE

The *popular* and *serious* slogans of chapters one through nine required careful dissection in the form of opening and middlegame strategy. In chapters ten through twenty, we'll collapse the opening and middlegame responses into one response that incorporates elements from both. Although these slogans are not as substantive as the others, we still want to be ready to respond to them.

As *faith* is the target of this slogan, we should start by asking what the objector means by that word. Also, know that debates over definitions can sometimes be contentious. That typically occurs when someone starts by accusing the other person of misrepresenting a position. Even if the person *is* misrepresenting a position, interactions arouse less friction when that is brought out with questions. That is why the **listen** portion of the **listen–reason–propose** framework is so critical.

Ask, **"What do you mean by faith and how did you come to that definition?"** Those pushing this slogan frequently characterize faith in one of the following ways:

- Belief without sufficient evidence
- Belief in spite of contrary evidence
- Pretending to know what you don't really know
- Just believing something without questioning it

But such conceptions of faith are seriously deficient. You might respond, "If that's what 'faith' means, then I agree with you it's problematic. But I don't think of faith that way." At that point, the person might ask, "Oh, what do you mean by faith, then?" That gives you a chance to **reason** and **propose** something more for their consideration. More on that in a moment.

Your interlocutor may present anecdotal evidence from his upbringing (or that of others), in which faith was understood in precisely those terms. He may say he was always told to "just have faith" and not ask too many questions. Your job is not to criticize such anecdotal evidence. Rather, it's an opportunity to sympathize and find common ground. You might say:

"I'm sorry that you were told to believe without evidence, and I've heard Christians say they, too, were told not to ask questions. But there's another side to the story. For 2000 years, people have been asking and answering difficult questions about faith. In the Catholic Christian tradition, we have sayings such as, 'faith seeking understanding,' and 'ten thousand difficulties do not make one doubt,' which point to how we can navigate difficult questions about faith without giving up on a belief in God."

Here's a follow-up question to ask: **"Have you considered any alternative definitions of faith?"** This gets the person thinking and reveals whether he has looked into possible Christian responses to his criticism. Also, it opens the door for you to provide an alternative definition of faith.

For Catholics, the following definition of faith comes to us from St. Thomas Aquinas: "Believing is an act of the intellect assenting to divine truth by command of the will moved by God through grace."[82] Put a different way, faith consists in *trusting what God has revealed,* since God is eminently trustworthy and cannot lie (CCC 156-157).

That definition might be off-putting to the skeptic, however. He may reply, "See! Faith is just a blind trust or willingness to believe something that you don't have evidence for!" But nothing in what we've laid out entails "blind trust" or belief without evidence.

Note that the descriptions of faith refer to "divine truth" or "what God has revealed." But how do we know what God has revealed? Or where he has revealed it? These are things that demand evidence. Or, as the *Catechism* puts it, the revelation of God is accompanied by various *motives of credibility*. These include miracles, prophesy, and the holiness of the saints. Why believe in Jesus or the Bible? Well, for starters, Jesus fulfilled prophecies in the Old Testament, rose from the dead, and established a Church that has verified many miracles over the centuries.

The goal at this step is not to present arguments and evidence for all that. Of course, the Resurrection and other miracles can be great topics later in the discussion.[83] The main point so far is this: **faith in the Catholic tradition does not require ignoring evidence, but rather it is normative for faith to be *accompanied* by evidence, that is, motives of credibility.** The First Vatican Council codifies this line of thought:

> However, in order that the "obedience" of our faith should be "consonant with reason" [cf. Rom. 12:1], God has willed that to the internal aids of the Holy Spirit there should be joined external proofs of his revelation, namely: divine facts, especially miracles and prophecies which, because they clearly show forth the omnipotence and infinite knowledge of God, are most certain signs of a divine revelation, and are suited to the intelligence of all (*De Filius* 3).

In addition to motives of credibility, there is a second reason in the Catholic tradition that faith is not irrational. Namely, that God's grace works in us to help us to have faith. *De Filius* continues:

> But the Catholic Church professes that this faith, which is the beginning of human salvation, is a supernatural virtue by which we, with the aid and inspiration of the grace of God, believe that the things revealed by him are true, not because the intrinsic truth of the revealed things has been perceived by the natural light of reason, but because of the authority of God himself who reveals them, who can neither deceive nor be deceived.

In other words, God helps us interiorly and provides grace at the level of our wills to make our faith firm and lasting. This further shows the rationality of faith, as it is in accord with right reason to cooperate with God's grace in accepting the testimony of the God who is Reason and Truth itself.

Of course, the atheist will deny this is possible, since he doesn't believe God exists. But that's not the point. At this stage, we are responding to the charge that faith is irrational. Our first point was to show that faith is not opposed to evidence. Second, we're arguing that *if God exists*, and helps us believe, then we have an additional reason that faith is not irrational. When we believe, we're doing what God wants us to do with the help of his grace.

At this point, you might introduce a question to make the point more vivid: **"If God exists, wouldn't it be rational to have faith in him and what he has revealed?"** Now, we know the atheist doesn't think God exists. However, we can still ask for speculation, and the skeptic can reason hypothetically that *if* God exists and has provided interior grace alongside external signs of his divine reality, then we should believe him and all that he reveals. Naturally, the conversation may turn to the motives of credibility or the evidence for God's existence. In that case, you can draw upon material from chapters 1, 21, and 22.

Questions to Ask

- "What do you mean by faith and how did you come to that definition?"
- "Have you considered any alternative definitions of faith?"
- "If God exists, wouldn't it be rational to have faith in him and what he has revealed?"

Important Principles

- Agree that *if* faith meant only belief without any evidence, then you would not endorse having that sort of faith.
- Explain that faith in the Catholic tradition is not irrational for two reasons:
  - Divine revelation is accompanied by motives of credibility that show it is reasonable to trust in what God has revealed.
  - God moves us interiorly, by grace, to assist us in the assent of faith.

Recommendations for Further Study

- Listen to these two podcast episodes where we discuss the topic of faith and whether it is irrational:

- "Is Faith Irrational?" with Lawrence Feingold.
  - www.classicaltheism.com/feingold.
- "Is Faith in Christ Irrational?" with Fr. Gregory Pine, O.P.
  - www.classicaltheism.com/pine.
- Read paragraphs 142 to 184 of the *Catechism of the Catholic Church*, which discuss the concept of faith in the Catholic tradition.
- Read the book *Faith Comes from What is Heard* by Lawrence Feingold (Steubenville, OH: Emmaus Academic, 2016).

11

"Religious belief is silly, childish, wishful thinking, an invention to quell our fear of death, a crutch, and/or the opiate of the masses."

Famous atheists have espoused these slogans. Karl Marx declared that religion is "the opiate of the masses." Sigmund Freud promoted the idea that "belief is wishful thinking." Some New Atheists dismiss belief in God as irrational or childish. And at a family funeral, one of my in-laws remarked, "Religion is a crutch for weak people that don't know how to deal with the difficulties of life." All these assertions purportedly point to serious deficiencies in religious belief. How might we respond?

OUR RESPONSE

I lump these slogans together because they can be dealt with in a similar way. The key response is this: none of these objections amount to showing that belief in God is false. They attempt to highlight a defect in religious belief, but if the belief is correct, the deficiencies evaporate.

More on that below. First, I'd start off with some simple questions, **"How did you come to that conclusion?"** or **"Why do you think that?"** Next, aim to show how the defect disappears if God exists.

Consider the idea that "belief is wishful thinking." If that is true, it is not *mere* wishful thinking. On the Catholic Christian worldview, God might create human beings with an instinct to wish for him. After all, knowing God in the beatific vision is the chief end of man, and if God is drawing men to himself (John 11:32), then we would expect people to long for and wish for him. So belief in God can be wishful *and* true. To drive this point home, ask, **"Isn't it possible that belief in God is wishful thinking because God made people to wish for him or have a deep longing for him?"**

Next, consider the claim that religion is "the opiate of the masses." Again, if belief in God is correct, this quip has no force. The mere fact that something reduces the suffering that many people feel as part of the human condition does not make it false or illicit. It's perfectly possible that God could want religious services and religious communities to offer people hope and love in the midst of suffering and hardship. If God is real and a religion is true, this would not be the false comfort that an opiate offers.

Ask a question to introduce the point: **"Isn't it possible that religion seems like a drug for the masses because God wanted it to be a remedy for pain and suffering?"**

Likewise the idea that religion is a "crutch," Crutches aid those who are injured. If God exists, then he is the crutch we need to lean on in troubled times. Also, Christianity holds that human beings are a fallen race and messed up badly by sin. In such a condition, they need spiritual medical attention, which makes the metaphor of a crutch even more appropriate. So this slogan too fails to provide a reason for atheism over theism. Let's use a question to make the point: **"Isn't it appropriate for us to have a crutch if we're part of an injured human race?"**

What about the charge that religion was invented to "quell our fear of death?" But if God exists, then it's true that he could conquer death by providing us with everlasting life. And it seems fitting that he would make us aware of his intention to do so. So that sub-slogan has no force if belief in God is correct.

Lastly, the person who says religious belief is irrational and childish needs to spell out his position more clearly. What does the objector mean when he says belief is childish or irrational? He probably has the *there is no evidence-for-God* objection in mind. If so, refer to the resources in chapter one. But to know what he has in mind, ask, **"Why do you think it's irrational or childish to believe in God?"** The atheist must explain his claim. That further explanation will constitute the actual objection. The *childish* and *irrational* labels simply give a polemical flavor to the slogan, but they do not provide the details of an argument we can engage. To find out those details, **ask questions**, then strive to implement our framework of **listen–reason–propose.**

What might this atheist have in mind when he says faith is "irrational" or "childish"? He probably considers faith to require a naïve gullibility. Just as a child might grow up believing in Santa Claus just because that is what he was told.

In reply, we can find some common ground by agreeing that blind, naïve gullibility is not a great way to get to the truth. As Catholics, we believe that faith is accompanied by motives of credibility and that God assists believers with his grace.

But at the heart of this critic's complaint is the idea that it's bad to believe in something because we were taught it at a young age—like Santa. But is this so? After all, if God exists, isn't it possible that he intends for truths about himself to be passed down to children from their parents? And surely we can all agree that parents and teachers should instruct children, from a young age, in many things that are good and true: for example, proper hygiene, or how to be generous and kind. Passing down certain things to children, then, and expecting children to adhere to them, is only bad if the things are harmful or untrue.

"Exactly right!" the skeptic could reply. "And faith is harmful and untrue because God does not exist."

Of course, such a response begs the question. And so you can focus on the real issue by asking, **"Why do you think that God doesn't exist? What are your reasons for that claim?"** After all, we have many good reasons to think that Santa Claus is not real, but no comparable reasons to think that God isn't.

By going through each one of these proposed deficiencies (wishful thinking, opiate of the masses, a crutch, childish, irrational, etc.) and explaining them in a theistic way, we show that these slogans do not point toward atheism. Rather, they fit a certain pattern that one Christian philosopher has identified with some specialized terminology.

In *Knowledge and Christian Belief*, Alvin Plantinga distinguishes *de jure* objections to Christian or theistic belief from *de facto* objections. In this chapter, we have focused exclusively on *de jure* objections. *De jure* objections purport to show that belief in God is in some way defective without necessarily aiming to show the belief is false. *De facto* objections target the truth of a belief and attempt to show that belief in God is false, and, conversely, that atheism is true. What I have illustrated here is a principle defended by Plantinga in detail: **there is no successful *de jure* objection independent of a *de facto* objection.** Unless someone targets the truth of belief in God or Christian belief, the *de jure* objections have no teeth.

In other words, labeling Christians as crowd-following, childish, wishful-thinking people does not show that their beliefs are false. The atheist must assume his burden of proof. He needs a *de facto* objection that shows belief in God is false. The most common *de facto* objections include evil and hiddenness, which we have already addressed. So you are well-equipped to answer this slogan!

Questions to Ask

- When someone proposes a defect in religious belief, ask, "How did you come to that conclusion?" or "Why do you think that?"

- In response to the claim that belief is wishful thinking, ask, "Isn't it possible that belief in God is wishful thinking because God made people to wish for him or have a deep longing for him?"

- In response to the claim that religion is the opiate of the masses, ask, "Isn't it possible that God wants religion to ease human pain and hardship?"

- In response to the idea that religion is a crutch, ask, "Isn't it appropriate for us to have a crutch if we're part of an injured human race?"

Important Principles

- Faith in the Catholic tradition is not blind, naïve gullibility.
- There is no *de jure* objection that works independently of a *de facto* objection.
- Since the phenomena in question can be well-explained *if God exists,* it does not constitute evidence for atheism over theism.

Recommendations for Further Study

- Read the book *Knowledge and Christian Belief* by Alvin Plantinga (Grand Rapids, MI: Eerdmans, 2015).

12

"Absence of evidence is evidence of absence" (Russell's Teapot).

A famous illustration frequently accompanies this slogan. God is just like a floating teapot in outer space for which we have no evidence. And this absence of evidence for God should be taken as evidence of his absence. The atheist Bertrand Russell put it like this:

> If I were to suggest that between the Earth and Mars there is a china teapot revolving about the sun in an elliptical orbit, nobody would be able to disprove my assertion provided I were careful to add that the teapot is too small to be revealed even by our most powerful telescopes. But if I were to go on to say that, since my assertion cannot be disproved, it is an intolerable presumption on the part of human reason to doubt it, I should rightly be thought to be talking nonsense. If, however, the existence of such a teapot were affirmed in ancient books, taught as the sacred truth every Sunday, and instilled into the minds of children at school, hesitation to believe in its existence would become a mark of eccentricity and

entitle the doubter to the attentions of the psychiatrist in an enlightened age or of the Inquisitor in an earlier time.

Russell's point is twofold. First, just because an assertion cannot be disproved, that is no good reason to think it is true. Second, that comprehensive inculturation could lead to belief in an interplanetary teapot just as it leads to belief in God. We will tackle the inculturation idea in chapter eighteen, "If you were born in Saudi Arabia, you'd be a Muslim." Here, we focus on the slogan in the chapter title and Russell's first claim.

OUR RESPONSE

First, note that the slogan assumes that there is no good evidence for God. In that respect, it is similar to the slogan in chapter one, "There's no evidence for God's existence," and we can offer similar responses.

Say to your discussion partner, **"It sounds like you're saying there is no evidence for God's existence. Is that part of your claim?"** If he says yes, then you can respond with the chapter-one question, **"What's the best evidence for God that you've come across and what do you think is wrong with it?"** Refer back to chapter one for the range of responses to expect.

Next, consider Russell's claim that "if I were to go on to say that, since my assertion cannot be disproved, it is an intolerable presumption on the part of human reason to doubt it, I should rightly be thought to be talking nonsense." Here we can agree with Russell that simply saying something cannot be disproved is not a reason to affirm it. If your interlocutor raises this issue, you can agree, and it provides a chance to find common ground in the discussion.

Now let's examine the slogan "absence of evidence is evidence of absence" in more detail. Consider an illustration that might be presented by a skeptic. We suspect someone might have cancer. Suppose the doctors do several tests and screenings and fail to find any evidence that the patient has cancer. Of course, this does not prove with absolute certainty that there is no cancer lurking somewhere. But the rational thing to believe is that the patient is cancer-free. In other words, the absence of evidence is evidence of absence.

How should we reply to that? In that case, absence of evidence *is* evidence of absence. However, the illustration allows us to clarify *under what conditions* evidence of absence counts as evidence of absence. William Lane Craig explains two conditions that must obtain:

1. We have thoroughly searched for evidence in all the appropriate areas.
2. We would expect to have more evidence than we do, in a given case.

The case of doctors testing for cancer and declaring the patient cancer-free satisfies. Doctors conducted thorough testing in appropriate areas, the first condition, and found no cancer. Second, if there were truly any cancer, we *would* expect it to show up on some of the medical tests. Since no evidence for cancer showed up, it's reasonable to conclude the patient is cancer-free. In this case, absence of evidence is evidence of absence.

Now, for atheists to use the slogan effectively, they must show that both conditions are met. In the case of the existence of God, absence of evidence is evidence of absence if and only if:

1. The atheist has fully canvassed the appropriate areas in philosophy and history. He has carefully inspected the arguments for God and shown why they fail.
2. We would expect to have more evidence than we do *if* in fact God exists.

After explaining the two conditions, ask, **"So, given those conditions, what's some of the evidence you've examined and how does it fail?"** This provides a chance for the skeptic to establish the first condition. However, if he provides only crude caricatures of theistic arguments or other weak evidence,[84] you can **propose** something better for his consideration. Also, in that case, the first condition is not met.

I contend that the atheist will fail to meet condition 1) because the evidence for God's existence and Jesus' resurrection is very good. However, to have a productive discussion you will need to study this evidence and prepare to present it. See appendices A and B for more on those specifics.

What can we say about condition 2)? Well, in order for this condition to be met we would supposedly need more evidence than the Kalam argument, the contingency argument, the moral argument, the fine-tuning argument, Aristotelian arguments, arguments for the resurrection of Jesus, arguments from religious experience, arguments from miracles, and many others It's hard to see why we must expect to have more than this plethora of evidence. Of course, none of that evidence might be convincing to someone who resists belief in God. A degree of hiddenness remains, yet these are very good reasons to think that God exists.

Questions to Ask

- "It sounds like you're saying there is no evidence for God's existence. Is that part of your claim?"
- "You say there's no evidence. I'm curious, what's the best evidence for God that you've come across and what do you think is wrong with it?"

Important Principles

- Absence of evidence only counts as evidence of absence if two conditions are met:
  - We have thoroughly searched for evidence in all the appropriate areas.
  - We would expect to have more evidence than we do, in a given case.

Recommendations for Further Study

- Watch this lecture by William Lane Craig: https://www.youtube.com/watch?v=_XZb8m7p8ng.

13

"Atheists are simply people who lack a belief in God. We don't have to prove that God doesn't exist."

The popularity of this slogan has exploded over the past decade. Traditionally, atheists said they believe that no gods exist and offered arguments for that claim. In our day, many popular atheists opt for the position that they merely *lack a belief in God*. As Dan Barker put it:

Atheism is not a belief that there is no God. Atheism is not a knowledge claim that there's no God. Some atheists, a small subset of atheists, will say, "Well I know there is no God," especially if he's defined a certain way. . . . Atheism is simply the absence of a belief. It's not a religion. It's not a creed. Atheism is the absence of belief in the same way that "off" is a TV channel . . . or in the same way that baldness is a hair color.[85]

This modern definition positions atheists in a more comfortable spot in two ways. First, it helps them be seen as open to evidence; they just haven't found it yet. Second, it puts a heavy burden of proof on theists: if a believer cannot show that God exists to a skeptic's satisfaction, the skeptic is the more rational one by sticking to his atheism. If you encounter atheists on the internet, it is likely they will express this form of atheism, which some have called "lack-theism."

OUR RESPONSE

Disputing the definition of atheism or arguing over who *really* has the burden of proof can quickly lead to a contentious exchange.[86] Instead, we should begin by asking questions that will lead back to examining the evidence. Our aim is not to compel skeptics to relinquish their definitions.[87] Rather, we want to **listen-reason-propose** and pray that the Holy Spirit uses our conversation to lead the atheist closer to God. So, what questions should we ask when someone presents the slogan in this chapter title?

First, you might ask, **"Did you always lack a belief in God? How did you come to this position?"** This allows you to gather more information from your discussion partner regarding his objections to religious belief. Maybe he had a traumatic personal experience. Maybe he stumbled upon intellectual difficulties he felt could not be overcome. By asking this question, you aim to find out what moved this person to embrace the atheist label.

Second, you might ask, **"Do you think that God does not exist? Why or why not?"** This question also allows the skeptic to present his reasons. Perhaps he has never met any theist who could offer an adequate case for

God's existence. That still would not imply that God does not exist. So if he thinks God does not exist, he may have additional reasons that we want to hear.

The goal of these initial questions is to find out *why* he thinks God does not exist (or that God's existence is unlikely). What pushed him into *atheism* as opposed to *agnosticism?*

Now, at some point, you may want to challenge his definition of *atheist,* but you should do so through questions. Here's one I find helpful, **"You say an atheist is someone who lacks a belief in God. So, on your view, what's the difference between an *atheist* and an *agnostic?"*** This requires him to clarify his position, since agnostics lack a belief in God as well. A common response is as follows:

"The term *agnostic* refers to one's knowledge and the term *atheist* refers to one's lack of belief. You can be an agnostic atheist or a gnostic atheist. The former lacks belief in God but doesn't claim to *know* that God does not exist. The latter lacks belief in God and claims to *know* that God does not exist. So on this understanding of the terms, I am an agnostic atheist." The following matrix of belief is often what this skeptic has in mind:

		Do you *know* your belief is true?	
		Yes	No
Do you *believe* that God exists?	Yes	Gnostic Theist	Agnostic Theist
	No	Gnostic Atheist	Agnostic Atheist

At this point, you should decide between two options. The first is to *engage* the matrix and attempt to clarify its terms in a way that leads to a productive exchange. The second is to *avoid* the matrix and ask questions to reframe the issue. Let's take each option in turn.

Suppose we want to engage the matrix. Proceed with caution. Sometimes, when defining these terms, skeptics will conflate "know" with "knowing with certainty." However, knowledge does not require 100 percent certainty to count as real knowledge. The skeptic may ask you to declare yourself an agnostic theist or gnostic theist. He may even ask, **"Do you really claim to *know* God exists?"** and scoff at you as intellectually dishonest if you give a simple yes.

As Catholic Christians, we do believe that God's grace working in the believer is capable of providing a firm certainty, known as the certainty of faith (CCC 157). Nonetheless, this can be confusing to unbelievers who do not think it's possible to be certain of much at all. Also, the certainty *of faith* lies in a different category than the certainty *of demonstrated knowledge*. The certainty *of faith* requires God's grace to move the will whereas the certainty *of demonstrated knowledge* can be attained by the natural light of human reason.

Nonetheless, the skeptic will likely not be aware of such Catholic teachings, and explaining them may lead to more confusion. So before answering where you lie on the matrix, you might answer the skeptic more tentatively: "I think I'd consider myself a gnostic theist, though it does depend how you're using the term *knowledge*. **What I want to say is that I think there are good reasons to believe God exists. Coupling that with my personal commitment to God in prayer and the sacraments, I've come to have a firm belief that God exists. But I don't claim to know God exists with the 100-per-**

cent certainty of demonstrated knowledge, as with a mathematical equation."

Now, the skeptic might respond, "That actually means you're an agnostic atheist." That seems like an odd way to use the label, but if that is how your dialogue partner understands the term, you can agree for the sake of moving the discussion forward.

Next, the conversation can naturally turn to those good reasons, and a chat about where the evidence points.

Return to the matrix and suppose you want to take option two: avoid the matrix and ask a question to reframe the issue. One danger with this path is that the atheist may accuse you of dodging a tough question. To avoid that situation, acknowledge his presentation of categories in your process of reframing: **"That's an interesting way of thinking about the terms. I have heard those before, but I haven't always found that way of breaking it down very helpful. Another way to look at the issue is to think about how you answer the question, Does God exist? If yes, then you're a theist. If no, then you're an atheist. Or, you could say 'I don't know' and be an agnostic. What do you think about that?"**

That could lead to a clearer answer about what this skeptic thinks. Regardless of which option you take to the matrix, the goal is to uncover *why* the person considers himself an atheist, and to move the conversation to those underlying reasons.

Another helpful question to ask on this front is, **"When you look at the reasons for and against God, where do you think the evidence points and why?"** That kind of question drives the discussion back to the evidence and allows you to offer something more for the person's consideration.

If you get stuck in a contentious spot regarding definitions and burdens of proof, don't be afraid to say something like this: **"Look, I'm sorry for misunderstanding your position. I don't know the ins and outs of atheism and burdens of proof, but I do think there are good reasons to believe in God. And I'm curious what your reasons are for holding to atheism. So what do you say about turning to that now instead?"** Skeptics may appreciate your honesty when you admit misunderstanding or lack of knowledge in some area. This reply can build rapport and lead to a more productive exchange of ideas, perhaps in a follow-up discussion.

WHO ACTUALLY HAS THE BURDEN OF PROOF?

The burden of proof rests on different parties in different contexts. In our criminal courts, the prosecution has the burden to show guilt; the defendant is presumed innocent until proven guilty. In discussions about competing world-views, a typical convention is that the burden of proof rests on whoever advances a claim. Yet, this can lead to an odd standoff where both sides refuse to advance claims out of a desire to avoid shouldering the burden of proof.

As I see it, there is no one-size-fits-all answer to whether theists or atheists have the burden of proof. Instead of debating who *really* has a burden, we should allow people to advance reasons for their worldviews and examine them. Here's an additional question you can ask an atheist: **"What do you think is the likelihood that God exists? Exact numbers here are not what I'm getting at, but I'm just curious if you see it as zero-percent likelihood or fifty-fifty or something else? And why?"** This will reveal more about why the skeptic thinks the way he does. An atheist who claims the likelihood is zero percent presents a stronger claim that one who says it's closer to fifty-fifty.[88] By listening to atheists' reasons for their worldview, we may have an opportunity to offer something more for their consideration regarding the rationality of theism.

Questions to Ask

- "Did you always lack a belief in God? How did you come to this position?"
- "Do you think that God does not exist? Why or why not?"
- "What's the difference between atheism and agnosticism on your view?"
- "When you look at the reasons for and against God, where do you think the evidence points and why?"
- "What do you think is the likelihood that God exists? Exact numbers here are not what I'm getting at, but I'm just curious if you see it as zero percent likelihood or fifty-fifty or something else?"

Important Principles

- Do not quibble about definitions or who has the burden of proof.
- When faced with the gnostic/agnostic/theist/atheist matrix, choose one of two options:
  - *Engage* the matrix and explain why you claim to be a gnostic theist.
  - *Avoid* the matrix and provide an alternative framing of the issue.

- If the discussion gets out of hand, don't be afraid to say this: "Look, I'm sorry for misunderstanding your position. I don't know the ins and outs of atheism and burdens of proof, but I do think there are good reasons to believe in God. And I'm curious what your reasons are for holding atheism. So what do you say about turning to that now instead?"

Recommendations for Further Study

- Read the book *Answering Atheism* by Trent Horn.
- For more specifics on the "Burden of Proof" issues, see this podcast episode with Thomas Bogardus: www.classicaltheism.com/burdenofproof

14

"*Real* philosophers don't take theistic arguments seriously."

Some people dismiss William Lane Craig and the cosmological argument, for example, as intellectually lightweight, based on some presumed consensus of academic philosophers having rejected it. Others may simply wave away St. Thomas Aquinas as irrelevant; famously, Richard Dawkins takes just a few pages to addresse Aquinas's "Five Ways" (five proofs for God) in *The God Delusion*.[89]

Such cavalier dismissals can even come from knowledgeable academics. For example, theoretical physicist Mano Singham criticized Edward Feser's *Five Proofs of the Existence of God* while admitting he had not read it. Singham writes:

> You would not need five arguments for god's [*sic*] existence if any one of them were really good. Although I have not read this book, I am slightly familiar with Feser's work and discussed six years ago an article he wrote about what it takes to be a Christian and why all the other religions are wrong. There too he disdained the need for any evidence and said that purely rational

arguments are sufficient. I have not read his new book and so can only guess at these proofs but going by the names that are dropped I can guess that they consist of warmed over versions of the prime mover, Kalam, design, and the ontological arguments.[90]

"Craig? Give me a break. You know all of his arguments have been refuted, right?" "Aquinas? Maybe ignorant medievals found him interesting but today we know better." How should we respond to such smug dismissals?

OUR RESPONSE

It's tempting to respond to sarcasm and smugness in like manner. But that's not the path we should take as Catholic Christians. In a memorable YouTube video, Fr. Mike Schmitz encourages Catholics to be unoffendable.[91] The reason is that when someone attacks us or makes a dismissive remark, either what they say is true or false. If it's false, then it cannot hurt us. And if it's true, then as Catholics called to live in the truth, we should not be offended by hearing it.

This does not mean there is no time or place for polemical speech or forceful criticism of another's position. But in the context of conversations with atheists whom we want to draw to the Faith, bringing a lot of attitude and polemics to the table is unhelpful. This is yet another reason why the principle *pray every day* is important, as God can guide us how to speak to others. With that out of the way, let's answer the slogan directly.

If someone says, "Real philosophy professors don't take the cosmological argument seriously," you should ask, **"How did you come to that conclusion?"** It's a very broad claim to make, and you want to hear their evidence.

And you can ask, **"Have you considered that many philosophers of religion, such as Edward Feser, Alexander Pruss, and Robert Koons, take the cosmological argument very seriously?"** This can lead to a discussion of the Kalam cosmological argument or a contingency argument for God's existence.

Next, let's answer Singham's point that we "would not need five arguments for god's existence if any one of them were really good." A silly objection. Ask a question to show why: **"What's the evidence for evolution? If there is evidence from homology, genetics, fossils, and other sources, should we suppose the evidence is no good because one source should be enough?"** Clearly, that philosophers have developed multiple arguments for God's existence is no more evidence of their weakness than that multiple sources of evidence for evolution show the weakness of that theory.

Similarly, mathematicians have developed dozens of proofs for the Pythagorean theorem. Yet, the multiplicity of proofs does not serve to undermine its truth; rather, proceeding along different paths (some algebraic, some geometric, and so forth), they reveal different aspects of it. There is nothing stopping arguments for God's existence from doing the same.

You might also offer the illustration of a trial in which you, as the lawyer, want to adduce all the evidence on behalf of your client. Even if you think one piece of evidence should seal the deal, you present multiple lines of evidence so that the jury can become further convinced of the conclusion you want them to come to. You should canvas *all* the best evidence for a view when considering its truth.

What about the way the slogan dismisses Thomas Aquinas, William Lane Craig, and others? How should we handle that? First, note that Aquinas's teachings are eminently defensible today, despite the supposed refutations, many of which are ill-informed. This applies to William Lane Craig as well. He has often won public debates against atheists; perhaps that is in part because his arguments were not as superficial and easy to refute as they thought.

Second, respond to the claim that the likes of Aquinas and Craig have been thoroughly refuted by asking, **"Can you explain the refutations?"** or **"How did you come to that conclusion?"** If your interlocutor offers a substantial argument against Aquinas, you should praise him for doing his homework. And if you *know* how to respond properly, you can offer something more for his consideration. If not, commend him for his study, and let him know you will look into the issue and get back to him.

However, it is more likely that your dialogue partner has not considered Aquinas, Craig, et al. seriously and has dismissed them too quickly.

I would again encourage honest conversation that leaves condescension aside. You can see your opponent's misunderstanding or quick dismissal as an opportunity to share something more for his consideration. A great book to recommend for a contemporary explanation and defense of many of St. Thomas's philosophical views is *Aquinas* by Edward Feser. For some of the best work of William Lane Craig, you might ask your dialogue partner to look into his book *Reasonable Faith: Christian Truth and Apologetics*, as well as his YouTube debates.

Questions to Ask

- "Can you explain the refutation?"

- "Have you considered that many philosophers of religion, such as Edward Feser, Alexander Pruss, and Robert Koons, take the cosmological argument very seriously?"

Important Principles

- A multiplicity of proofs does not imply the weakness of a belief or theory (e.g., evolution and the Pythagorean theorem).

- Referencing a refutation is not the same as providing a refutation.

- Recommend the book *Aquinas: A Beginner's Guide* by Edward Feser.

Recommendations for Further Study

- Read *Aquinas: A Beginner's Guide* by Edward Feser (London: Oneworld Publications, 2009).

- Read *Faith and Reason: Philosophers Explain Their Turn to Catholicism* (San Francisco: Ignatius Press, 2019).

  - In the chapter by Feser, he lists six common misunderstandings about Aquinas's work that lead many to think his arguments have been refuted.

  - Also, this book contains a chapter by the natural theologian and philosopher Robert Koons, who is one of the people we mentioned who takes cosmological arguments seriously.

- Listen to this podcast episode on "Logical Pointers" with Bryan Cross: http://www.classicaltheism.com/cross.

MISCELLANEOUS SLOGANS

15

"If we burned all the science and religious books, only the science books would come back the same after a thousand years."

The actor Ricky Gervais used this slogan during an interview with late-night host (and professed Catholic) Stephen Colbert.[92]

> **Gervais:** Science is constantly proved all the time. You see, if we take something like any fiction, any holy book, and any other fiction, and destroyed it, in a thousand years' time, that wouldn't come back just as it was. Whereas if we took every science book, and every fact, and destroyed them all, in a thousand years they'd all be back, since all of the same tests would [give] the same results.
>
> **Colbert:** That's good. That's really good.

It's not entirely clear what the slogan is meant to show, but I think it's that religious claims are deficient and rely on gullibility whereas scientific claims are sound because they rely on empirical evidence. So the scientific method is a robust and accurate way of finding truth, and therefore scientific books would come back the same. On the other hand, religious truths fail this repeatability test.

OUR RESPONSE

Since the slogan's force is not altogether clear, the usual clarification question should be your first move: **"What exactly is this supposed to show?"** After that, I think you can give a short reply, in the manner in which Trent Horn tackled the slogan on Twitter in 2019. He responded to someone who made a similar claim by pointing out that if all *history* books were destroyed, the truths they contained wouldn't "come back" either. "A truth," he said, "is not disproven merely because it can't be rediscovered. Come on atheists, you can do better."

This objection also whiffs of scientism (that scientific research is the only way to genuine knowledge), which we addressed in chapter three. Perhaps this slogan can lead into a further conversation, though, about what counts as evidence and how we know that God exists. Perhaps you and the skeptic can agree that by itself this slogan shows nothing at all.

- Ask, **"What exactly is this supposed to show?"**
- Point out that if the reasoning is valid, the destruction of historical records would also disprove historical facts.

16

"Do you take the Bible literally? Hahahaha!"

This shallow slogan (or taunt) implies that no one today can take the Bible seriously—because the theory of evolution has overthrown our understanding of Genesis, because it's full of miracle stories, because it's thousands of years old, or whatever. How can we respond?

OUR RESPONSE

Whether or not one takes the Bible literally does nothing to show whether atheism is true. God's existence and the Bible being read literally (or not) are not mutually exclusive ideas. Perhaps God exists and *none* of the Bible should be taken literally. Of course, we do not believe that as Catholic Christians, but the point is that this slogan does not support atheism. Nonetheless, let's discuss an answer we can give that fits with our worldview.

Here's a response that I stole from Bishop Robert Barron. Say this, **"That's a good question. Let me ask you a question: do you take the library literally?"**

The proper answer to that question is: *it depends*. Some books in the library are taken literally, depending on their genre and context. Others are read figuratively. So it is with Sacred Scripture.

The Bible contains many types of writing: history, poetry, parables, proverbs, teaching epistles, and so forth. Whether we take a given passage literally depends on its genre and context.[93]

Moreover, we can say, sometimes it is unclear whether the author intends the reader to take a passage literally, and this tactical answer will help you avoid looking like a rigid literalist.

Keep in mind, we do not want to answer in such a way that the atheist thinks we don't take the Bible seriously. As Catholic Christians, we believe the Bible is God speaking, and we affirm that all that Scripture teaches is true.[94] However, we do not equate taking Scripture seriously with taking Scripture literally. Use a question to introduce this point: **"Isn't it possible to take a Scripture passage seriously without taking it literally?"** Then, you can offer an example.

Jesus teaches, "Whoever comes to me and does not hate father and mother, wife and children, brothers and sisters, yes, and even life itself, cannot be my disciple" (Luke 14:26). Of course, such language should not be construed literally, as it would contradict the commandment to honor mother and father. Instead, Jesus uses hyperbole to make the point that God must be first in our lives and we must love him above all things. And *that* teaching is something we take very seriously as Catholics.

Another question that arises when you make the points above: "If you take only some of the Bible literally, how do you decide which parts to take literally?" The implication is that Christians will just throw out the literal interpretation of any verse that raises a difficulty.

But we don't, or at least we shouldn't. Instead, we can rely on Bible commentators, historians, Sacred Tradition, and the Magisterium to help us know when, and to what extent, Scripture should be taken literally or not. Large portions of Scripture are clear in this regard. For example, the four Gospels and the Acts of the Apostles contain authentic history, plus theological pronouncements and moral teachings. The Psalms contain Hebrew poetry expressing worship, lamentation, repentance, and other things that capture the religious spirit of the Jews.

Some portions of Scripture require more analysis than others to discern their genre, authorial intent, and spiritual application. But that in no way implies that the Bible ought not to be taken seriously.

The Magisterium provides guidance for interpreting the Bible authentically. In many cases, theologians are free to propose interpretations and debate them, within the boundaries set by the Church. The work of biblical scholars and the Church is to interpret the Word of God in its proper context and apply it "for the sake of our salvation" (*Dei Verbum* 11).

Questions to Ask

- "Do you take the library literally?"
- "Isn't it possible to take a Scripture passage seriously without taking it literally?"

Principles and Examples

- The Bible is a library of books with a wide variety of different genres and contexts.

- It's possible to take the Bible seriously without taking it literally.
- Use the example of Jesus instructing us to "hate father and mother" to be his disciple.
- Bible commentators, Sacred Tradition, and the Magisterium can assist us when it comes to discerning how to read particular Scripture passages.

Recommendations for Further Study

- Read *A Catholic Introduction to the Bible: The Old Testament* by Brant Pitre and John Bergsma (San Francisco: Ignatius Press, 2018).
- Read *Hard Sayings* by Trent Horn.

17

"The Bible supports slavery!"

The triumvirate of complaints about the Bible from atheists typically consists of denouncing its science, denouncing its God, and denouncing its morality. In chapter three we dealt with scientific objections. In chapter nine we dealt generally with labeling God as an evil maniac. Here we'll handle a classic moral objection: the Bible is an evil book because it supports slavery (thus disproving Christianity and theism by implication).

In 2012, Dan Savage gave a keynote speech at a conference for high school journalists about bullying. One can find the viral clip where he proclaims that we should ignore the "[B.S.] in the Bible" on a variety of things. At one part of the presentation, he says this:

> We can learn to ignore the [B.S.] in the Bible about gay people. The same way, the same way we have learned to ignore the [B.S.] in the Bible about shellfish, about slavery, about dinner, about farming, about menstruation, about virginity, about masturbation. We ignore [B.S.] in the Bible about all sorts of things. The Bible is a radically pro-slavery document. Slave owners waved Bibles

over their heads during the Civil War and justified it. The shortest book in the New Testament is a letter from Paul to a Christian slave owner about owning his Christian slave. And Paul doesn't say "Christians don't own people." Paul talks about how Christians own people.

We ignore what the Bible says about slavery, because the Bible got slavery wrong. Tim—uh, Sam Harris, in *A Letter to a Christian Nation*, points out that the Bible got the easiest moral question that humanity has ever faced wrong.[95]

OUR RESPONSE

Even a quick examination of the New Testament and the letter to Philemon shows that Savage misses the mark in his interpretation. St. Paul exhorts Philemon to grant freedom to his slave Onesimus. In a key passage of the letter, Paul says:

Perhaps this is why he was parted from you for a while, that you might have him back for ever, *no longer as a slave but more than a slave, as a beloved brother,* especially to me but how much more to you, both in the flesh and in the Lord. So *if you consider me your partner, receive him as you would receive me* (15-17, emphasis mine).

It's true that Paul doesn't use the phrase, "Christians don't own people," but he doesn't have to say that to teach that slavery is no longer acceptable. It is plain from his teaching here, as well as in his other letters, that Christ has ushered in a law of love and that Christians ought to live by that love in how they treat others. Savage twists Paul's teaching to make it seem like it condones slavery when it does not. That's a specific example you may want to memorize when discussing slavery in the Bible.

But this is not the main challenge we face. Skeptics will insist that the Old Testament is full of rules for buying and owning slaves, and it never gives a hint that such an institution is wrong. Since it got this easy moral teaching wrong, it's untrustworthy in everything else.

Although this slogan does not directly argue against God's existence, it is typically put forward as a kind of circumstantial proof, as well as to make Christians uncomfortable, and so we want to have some additional answers.

To answer this challenge well, you should be able to do two things. First, draw important distinctions about biblical slavery. Second, explain specifics surrounding particularly difficult passages.[96] We will lay the groundwork for that first task, which can generally then be employed to address the difficult passages.

"Slavery" in the Old Testament context does not mean what most people today, especially in America with the evils of slavery in its not-too-distant past, have in mind. There are at least three different ways to use the term.

1. There is the "chattel slavery" that most people call to mind, which involves forcing people into service indefinitely, unwavering cruelty, and the reduction of people to mere property. Although this was common in the African-American slave trade (and gravely wrong), it's not what the Old Testament describes.

2. Old Testament slavery commonly refers to a process of indentured servitude that the poor and destitute (or those with enormous debts) would make use of temporarily. They could "sell themselves" as servants ("slaves") to pay off a debt or obtain sustenance for themselves and their families in a time and place with no government

welfare programs. Although this type of "slavery" is a hard thing to experience, it is not intrinsically wrong.

3. Sometimes "slavery" refers to *penal servitude* in which where wrongdoers are punished with forced labor. This is also not wrong in itself (even today, some criminal punishments include "community service"), although depending on circumstances it may not always be prudent.

People objecting to biblical slavery rarely make these distinctions, so we must. Reveal these distinctions to the skeptic, and you will enhance the conversation. Ask, **"Have you considered that the word *slave* or *servant* can be understood in several ways?"** Point out that in the Old Testament it usually refers to indentured servitude.

Even after hearing these distinctions, a skeptic may press two additional objections:

1. Why didn't Jesus condemn slavery in the New Testament?
2. But there are passages that clearly refer to the practice of chattel slavery.

Let's address each of those objections in turn.

"Why didn't Jesus condemn slavery?"

We could say first that Jesus had a greater purpose than eliminating slavery or any other particular social evil. His mission transcended *all* social and political issues. He came not to be the perfect political leader that some were expecting, but rather the Messiah who would "save his people from their sins" (Matt. 1:21).

This messianic mission of proclaiming God's kingdom, fulfilling the law, sacrificing himself out of love for us, rising from the dead, and ascending into heaven was more important in God's providential plan than correcting social institutions of a particular time and place. And although Jesus did not turn a blind eye to slavery, as we'll see, his core mission transcended the ins and outs of Roman politics.

Next, we must note that Christ's teaching to love God above all things and to love our neighbors as ourselves *does* mean that the practice of chattel slavery is intrinsically wrong. He may not have laid out a policy plan against slavery in particular, but he spoke plainly and powerfully about a way of love that is incompatible with chattel slavery.

"But there are passages that clearly refer to the practice of chattel slavery."

Consider this often-raised excerpt from the book of Leviticus:

> You shall not rule over him with harshness, but shall fear your God. As for your male and female slaves whom you may have: you may buy male and female slaves from among the nations that are round about you. You may also buy from among the strangers who sojourn with you and their families that are with you, who have been born in your land; and they may be your property (25:43-45).

Certainly, the atheist alleges, that is chattel slavery and the Bible plainly condones it!

We need to make several points to put the passage in context. The life of ancient Israelites was *far removed* from our modern way of life and we must fight the temptation to foist our own perspective upon the text.

First, none of the "slaves" of the Old Testament could be forced into labor through kidnapping. Exodus 21:16 expressly forbids kidnapping people to keep or sell as slaves, making such acts punishable by death. When other passages speak of "buying" slaves, people may assume that these were auctions of kidnapped slaves held against their will, as with African slaves in the mid-nineteenth century. But in fact even the "buying" of slaves included a voluntary element more akin to indentured servitude.

Second, as we noted, slaves often sold themselves into servitude as a form of survival. In the New International Bible Commentary, F.F. Bruce points out, "As was the case generally in the Near East, freeborn citizens most frequently fell into slavery through poverty and insolvency."[97]

One can find scriptural support for what Bruce describes in Genesis 47:13, where Joseph's brothers come to him begging to become his slaves due to their poverty and hunger: "Why should we die before your eyes, both we and our land? *Buy us and our land for food*, and we with our land will *be slaves* to Pharaoh; and give us seed, that we may live, and not die, and that the land may not be desolate" (Gen. 47:19, emphasis mine). The brothers beg to be "be slaves" to preserve their lives.

Third, just because the Bible regulates slavery doesn't mean the Bible endorses slavery in an unqualified way. The importance of this point can't be understated. In a way similar to how Moses allowed and regulated divorce for pragmatic reasons without thereby approving of it, the Bible regulated the existing practice of slavery (mostly indentured servitude). The biblical laws regulating slavery made the institution much more humane and respectful of the dignity of persons than in any other ancient Near-Eastern culture (they all practiced slavery in some form). So the Bible takes a gradual approach to the slavery question: first regulating it and making it more humane and later exhorting Christian slave owners to free their slaves.

Those pushing the slogan may still insist that the word *property* in Leviticus 25 *has* to imply chattel slavery. For a more detailed analysis and exegesis, I recommend two books at the end of this chapter, but here are a few of my own thoughts on the matter.

Again, the objector may be reading the word *property* here with American Southern slavery in mind. But I suggest that the notion of "property" was actually broad enough for the writer of Leviticus to include things that we might not deem appropriate today but are not equivalent to chattel slavery. An example can help support this. In Exodus 20, we see a presentation of the Ten Commandments, and in verse seventeen it says, "You shall not covet your neighbor's house; you shall not covet your neighbor's wife, or his manservant, or his maidservant, or his ox, or his ass, or anything that is your neighbor's."

Notice the listing of things not to covet: neighbor's *house*, neighbor's *wife*, neighbor's *servants*, and anything that is his (that is, his *property*). Ought we to conclude that the writer intends to put all things on this list in the same category? No. Especially since we learn from the opening chapters of Genesis that God creates both male and female in his image. Houses and other property do not bear the image of God. Yet, in the statement of Exodus 20:17, all of those things could be put together with a possessive description that does not require diminishing the dignity of wives or servants; they are not reduced to objects of possession like houses or animals. Similarly, the writer in Leviticus, who tradition tells us is Moses, could use the phrasing "and they may be your property" in such a way that does not entail chattel slavery.

At this point you may be accused of exegetical gymnastics. In that event, you can still stand on two solid points: 1) No matter how repugnant these descriptions are to modern ears, it is entirely plausible to read them as *regulatory* rather than *obligatory* and 2) We don't have to assume that the word used by the ancient author of this verse in Leviticus carried with it the exact same significance it bears today.

Questions to Ask

- "Have you considered that the biblical word *slave* or *servant* can be understood in several ways?"
- "Have you considered that Jesus did implicitly condemn slavery by his teachings on love?"

Important Principles

- Slavery can be understood in several senses and not all of them are intrinsically wrong. The slavery of the Old Testament most frequently refers to indentured servitude.
- None of the "slaves" regulated by the Old Testament could be acquired through kidnapping.
- "Slaves" sold themselves as servants in order to preserve their lives and those of their families.
- Just because the Bible *regulates* slavery does not mean it *recommends* slavery.
- The way things are phrased by an ancient writer do not necessarily mean what a modern reader calls to mind.

Recommendations for Further Study

- *Hard Sayings: A Catholic Approach to Answering Bible Difficulties* by Trent Horn.
- *Is God a Moral Monster?* by Paul Copan.

18

"If you were born in Saudi Arabia, you'd be a Muslim."

In 2006, Richard Dawkins used a variant of this slogan in response to an audience question:

> You're not a Muslim. You're not a Hindu. Why aren't you a Hindu? Because you happen to be brought up in America, not in India. If you had been brought up in India, you'd be a Hindu. If you'd been brought up in Denmark in the time of the Vikings you'd be believing in Wotan and Thor.[98]

In other words, geography and happenstance determine someone's religious beliefs; therefore, we cannot rationally hold them to be true. How should we respond?

OUR RESPONSE

This slogan purports to be an *undercutting defeater* for the theist. In philosophy, a "defeater" is a reason given against a certain belief. Alvin Plantinga distinguishes two types of defeaters:

Defeaters are reasons for giving up a belief B that you hold. If they are also reasons for believing B is false, they are rebutting defeaters; if they *aren't* reasons forbelieving B is false, they are undercutting defeaters.[99]

So why is the slogan an undercutting defeater as opposed to a rebutting defeater? Well, the slogan does not show, or claim to show, that God does not exist or that Christianity is false. The following facts may all be true simultaneously:

- People tend to inherit their religious beliefs.
- Few Christians live in Saudi Arabia as compared to Europe and America.
- Christianity is true.

These claims are not logically inconsistent. Since they can all be true at once, the slogan itself does not constitute a rebutting defeater for the Christian. Still, an atheist may insist that if the only reason someone believes in Christianity is by the accident of birth, then such a belief is unjustified. It amounts to just dumb luck. How can we respond to this line of reasoning?

First, let's ask a question that helps expose the underlying problem of the objection: **"Do you believe in equal rights for women and homosexuals?"**[100] When he answers yes, as is likely, ask a follow-up: **"Well if you were born in Saudi Arabia, you wouldn't believe in equal rights. You only believe in equal rights because you were brought up in America. Right?"**

At this point, your interlocutor may adduce other reasons for believing in equal rights. He may argue that it's not *merely* the fact of being born in America that makes him a believer in equal rights. Rather, he has given the issue serious thought and decided that supporting equal rights is the right thing to do.

Yet, the Catholic Christian can offer a similar reply. It's not *merely* the fact of being born in America that makes him a Catholic. Rather, he has given the issue serious thought and decided that the Faith is true. This can lead to a discussion of what that serious thought is, and the evidence for Catholic Christianity.

Some may find it worth mentioning that this slogan commits the *genetic fallacy*, which refers to the error of invalidating a belief by finding fault with *how* a person came to hold it, rather than showing why the belief is false. So you might press the objector with a related question: **"Isn't it possible that a person could come to hold a true belief through a faulty process? And if that's the case, should we not simply look at the belief itself and reasons for and against it?"**

One can also turn the tables on the secular skeptic by asking, **"The only reason you're a secular skeptic is that you were born in America. If you'd been born in India, you'd be a Hindu, right?"** If the skeptic answers yes, then he has put himself in an awkward position. If the accident-of-birth objection really shows a belief is false or unjustified, then it has just shown his own atheism is false or unjustified.

However, the skeptic probably will not answer yes, since he has other reasons to support his atheism. As Catholic Christians, we can do the same. We are not Catholic *merely* because of how and when we were born, but for additional reasons and our relationship with Jesus Christ.

BUT WHAT ABOUT THOSE WHO
HAVE NOT HEARD?

Another objection lurks in the background of discussions about religion being dictated by the accident of birth. In particular, if salvation depends on hearing and responding to the gospel, then what about those who never get a chance to hear it? It seems unfair for them to be consigned to hell for a failure to respond to something they never heard. How can we address this?

Christians have responded differently to this question. Typically, Catholics lead with the following thesis: All men are given sufficient grace to be saved, such that only those who reject God's grace and persist in sin will be lost. In the case of those who never hear the gospel, they can respond to God's grace as it is revealed to them through nature and conscience. If they come to be saved, such salvation comes through Christ and his Church, since the graces applied to them were merited by Christ on the cross.[101]

Some apologists have postulated further ideas to address the situation of those who have not heard the gospel. William Lane Craig has proposed the following: Suppose God has providentially ordered the world such that those who *would* respond to the gospel will be born at a time and place when they *will* hear it. In other words, on this hypothesis, it may be possible that no one is lost for failing to respond to the gospel, since all the people who would respond are given the chance to hear it. For those who do not hear the gospel, it may be the case that they would not have responded positively *even if* they had heard it.

Now, I do not necessarily endorse this hypothesis, as it seems to be based on the Molinist teaching of *middle knowledge*, which is somewhat controversial.[102] Middle knowledge refers to the view that God's omniscience includes knowing all counterfactuals of creaturely freedom—that is, what every individual *would* do in any possible circumstance. Nonetheless, I find this to be a helpful idea to put forward as a *possibility* for how the objection can be resolved. It should at least give the atheist some food for thought.

So when handling the question, "What about those who have not heard?" remember those two key points: 1) God gives all men sufficient grace to be saved, and 2) God may have providentially ordered the world so that no one is lost due to an unfair accident of birth.

Questions to Ask

- "Do you believe in equal rights for women and homosexuals?"

- "Well, if you were born in Saudi Arabia, you wouldn't believe in equal rights. You only believe in equal rights because you were brought up in America. Right?"

- "The only reason you're a secular skeptic is that you were born in America. If you'd been born in India, you'd be a Hindu, right?"

Important Principles

- Just as you can believe in equal rights for reasons apart from the accident of birth, you can have religious convictions apart from the accident of birth.

- You cannot invalidate a belief merely by criticizing *how* someone came to hold the belief. This is called the *genetic fallacy.*

- God provides all men sufficient grace to be saved. Those with no direct knowledge of Christian revelation could come to be saved by responding to God's grace as they come to understand it through nature and conscience. In such a case, they will still be saved *by Christ* and *through the Church*.

- Some postulate that God may have providentially ordered the world such that those who *would* respond to the gospel will be born at a time and place when they *will* hear it.

Recommendations for Further Study

- See Jon McCray's YouTube video for a good response to this slogan: https://www.youtube.com/watch?v=oE1a-TuQ8J4.

19

"If everything has a cause, then what caused God?"

Often this slogan is wielded after a theist uses a cosmological argument. The skeptic points out that God is made an arbitrary exception to the causal principle. Surprisingly, both philosophically engaged atheists and popularizers have offered this slogan in one form or another.[103] In his book *Breaking the Spell,* the atheist Daniel Dennett writes, "The Cosmological Argument . . . in its simplest form states that since everything must have a cause the universe must have a cause—namely, God."[104] From which follows the question posed by the title of this chapter, which can be stated as follows:

"You argue that everything needs a cause. But if that's the case, then what caused God? You say he doesn't need a cause, but that's an arbitrary exception. I could just say the universe doesn't need a cause either. That's why these cosmological arguments are all destined to fail. They boil down to arbitrary exceptions."

How should we answer this?

OUR RESPONSE

First, point out that the slogan is based on a straw-man version of the cosmological argument. In fact, none of the famous defenders of cosmological arguments—such as Aristotle, Averroes, Aquinas, and Leibniz—make use of the premise that everything has a cause.

So ask, **"Who said everything has a cause?"** If the skeptic answers, "Aquinas did!" (or someone else), then ask, **"Can you let me know *where* Aquinas (or other thinker) argues that way?"**

Then follow up by asking, **"Have you considered that the Kalam cosmological argument [or contingency argument] does not employ such a premise?"** Explain that real versions of cosmological arguments are not based on the premise that *everything* has a cause. Rather, they point to particular features of things that suggest they need a cause.

For example, in the Kalam cosmological argument, the major premise is as follows: Everything that begins to exist has a cause. In other words, the premise homes in on a particular feature of things; i.e., that they *begin* to exist. Things that fulfill that condition require a cause. But such a principle is silent as to those things which do not fulfill it. So, we can run the Kalam cosmological argument without making use of the premise embedded in the slogan:

Premise 1: Everything that begins to exist has a cause.

Premise 2: The universe began to exist.

Conclusion: Therefore, the universe has a cause.

Likewise, contingency arguments do not employ the general premise *everything has a cause*. Some explain contingency in terms of "dependence"; that is, that things that are dependent need a cause. Others may explain contingency as "needing an explanation," such that all contingent things need some causal explanation. Regardless of how a contingency argument is formulated, it will not rest on the premise that everything has a cause.[105]

So this slogan turns out not to be all that relevant. Quick clarification and questioning will reveal that no serious cosmological argument relies on the premise *everything has a cause*.

Questions to Ask:

- "Who said everything has a cause?"

- If someone says that Aquinas (or someone else) did, then ask, "I'm not sure that's right, but I'm willing to be corrected. Can you let me know *where* Aquinas (or other thinker) argues that way?"

- "Have you considered that the Kalam cosmological argument [or contingency argument] does not employ such a premise?"

Important Principles

- The correct way to formulate the causal premise of the Kalam or contingency argument singles out some feature of things as the reason they must have a cause.

  - For the Kalam argument, everything that *begins* to exist has a cause.

  - For a contingency argument, you might say everything *that is dependent on other things* requires a cause. Or, everything *that requires an explanation of its existence* needs a cause.

Recommendations for Further Study

- See chapter seven of Feser's *Five Proofs of the Existence of God* for a definitive treatment of this slogan.

20

"Religion is the cause of most wars and violence."

This claim has been repeated by many New Atheists. In *The End of Faith,* Sam Harris remarks that religion is "the most prolific source of violence in our history."[106] And in a witty take on the Ten Commandments, comedian George Carlin said:

> Murder. The Fifth Commandment. But, if you give it a little thought, you realize that religion has never really had a problem with murder. Not really. More people have been killed in the name of God than for any other reason.
>
> To cite a few examples, just think about Northern Ireland, the Middle East, the Crusades, the Inquisition, our own abortion-doctor killings and, yes, the World Trade Center to see how seriously religious people take Thou Shalt Not Kill. Apparently, to religious folks—especially the truly devout—murder is negotiable. It just depends on who's doing the killing and who's getting killed.

Although this slogan does not deny the existence of God, it can often be a gateway to other atheistic arguments. So we should be prepared to answer the person who declares that religion is the cause of most wars and violence.

OUR RESPONSE

First, let's suppose the slogan is true. It still does not do anything to show that God does not exist. To bring this out, simply ask, **"Is it possible for people to misuse religion to fight wars?"** To which the reply should be, "Of course!" Just because religion can be misused does not mean that it is false.

After all, most will be familiar with Jesus' teachings to love God above all things and love your neighbor as yourself (Matt. 22: 37-39). All cruelty and injustice in war is condemned by this teaching. Of course, it leaves open the question as to whether there is such a thing as "just war." The Catholic Church teaches there can be a just war under specific conditions (CCC 2307-2314).

But might not some leaders abuse just-war theory to go to war with base motives? Undoubtedly. But just because a theory can be misused does not mean it is false. And again, even if men sometimes go to war for unjust reasons but in the name of religion, that would not discredit religion itself.

Some atheists might be worried that just-war conditions are so nebulous that any religious leader could easily argue that a particular war is just even if it is not. In response, point out that the conditions for a just war are so difficult to demonstrate that Pope John Paul II and Pope Benedict XVI doubted whether such conditions could be met in most modern circumstances. Pope Benedict XVI said, "To say nothing of the fact that, given the new weapons that make possible destructions that go beyond the combatant groups, today we should be asking ourselves if it is still licit to admit the very existence of a 'just war.'"[107]

Next you might ask, **"Is it possible for a secular leader to promote unjust wars and violence?"** Of course, the answer is yes. In history, we have seen horrible atrocities carried out by explicitly atheistic regimes. The Reign of Terror following the French Revolution and the Soviet Union's totalitarian mistreatment of its citizens come to mind. Yet, we would not argue that secular leaders could not act justly. In other words, if the misuse of a worldview points to its falsehood, secular atheism fares no better than religion.

Next, let's question the accuracy of the slogan itself. Is it really true that religion is the cause of most wars and violence? If body count is the standard, the twentieth century fares horribly for atheism. Atheistic regimes in China and Russia are responsible for many millions of deaths.

Also, the causes of various wars are hotly debated by historians. Given that, is it easy to trace most wars to religious causes? Recent work on the subject suggests it is not. In their *Encyclopedia of Wars*, Charles Phillips and Alan Axelrod maintain that only about 123 out of 1,763 wars in history were religious in nature.[108] That amounts to about 7 percent, so the vast majority were *not* religious in nature. This turns the tables on the skeptic's claim. Ask, **"Have you considered that according to the *Encyclopedia of Wars*, only about 7 percent of them were religious in nature?"**

Ultimately, this slogan is a red herring. Even if religion can be misused, that does not mean it is false. Similarly, misused atheism does not prove atheism false. Ask questions to get at this fundamental point. If necessary, present the encyclopedia information on the proportion of wars that were religious in nature. All this should be more than enough to dissolve the force of the slogan and get to a more substantive discussion of good reasons to believe in God. It is that subject to which we now turn in part three.

Questions to Ask

- "Is it possible for people to misuse religion to fight unjust wars?"
- "Is it possible for a secular leader to promote unjust wars and violence?"
- "Have you considered that according to the *Encyclopedia of Wars*, only about 7 percent of them were religious in nature?"

Important Principles

- Just because religion can be misused does not mean it is false.
- Explain that according to the *Encyclopedia of Wars*, only about 7 percent of the wars in all of history have been religious in nature.

Recommendations for Further Study

- Read the article "Is Religion the Cause of Most Wars?" by Brett Kunkle, https://www.str.org/blog/is-religion-the-cause-of-most-wars#.XaG3_-dKiRs.

How to Present Evidence and Why Some Resist It

Most of this book focuses on how to respond to various slogans and atheistic arguments. When it comes to dealing with the top skeptical one-liners, we want to anticipate common objections and react appropriately. I hope chapters one through twenty gave you the groundwork to do just that. Still, something would be missing if we did not spend some time developing an *offensive* strategy. After all, our dialogue partner may truly be wondering: What are some *good reasons* to think God exists?

So, how can we argue for God? What should go into our *positive* case? How can we *propose* the evidence effectively? What arguments actually work? And why do some people resist evidence for God's existence? In appendices A and B of this book, I aim to answer these questions.

In this appendix, I recommend **seven tips** for presenting the evidence for God's existence and give **six reasons** why some resist it.

Tip 1: Stick to the *listen-reason-propose* framework.

In an emotionally charged world, it's tempting to respond to personal attacks in kind. Yet aggressive responses often generate more heat than light, while making the evangelistic ground less fertile.

As a math education major in college, I was introduced to the education guru Harry Wong, who had a helpful saying for teachers regarding everything we did in the classroom: "If you don't have a plan, you're planning to fail." In almost a decade of teaching, I've found this to be true. I have always made my worst decisions when I reacted on the spot to something I had not anticipated.

In your encounters with atheists and skeptics, you want to have a plan that prevents you from getting sucked into emotional reactions or spewing personal venom. That's why I recommend the **listen-reason-propose framework as a default plan. Of course, it may not apply smoothly to every situation, but you can force yourself to start with that approach.**

To listen well, ask good questions to clarify what your discussion partner has in mind. Craft questions that can lead the person to see things you deem worth seeing. Throughout this book, I've suggested questions for particular situations, but you can develop your own bank of questions to draw from and test out in conversation.

To reason well, provide examples and principles that reveal important truths about the topic under discussion. To **propose** something more for your discussion partner's consideration, ask, "Have you ever considered x, y, or z?" when you lay out an argument or piece of evidence. Use good examples and principles to help them understand the points worth seeing. So that's the first tip: **stick to the *listen-reason-propose* framework.**

Tip 2: Aim to find common ground.

You want your dialogue partner to be comfortable agreeing with you. This builds trust and softens the soil for more evidence to land well. You can do this even while disagreeing with the person's conclusion. Here's an example.

Suppose an atheist says, "Religious belief is irrational and childish. It's Santa Claus for adults. I don't want to believe things just because they sound nice." Now, we answered a slogan like this in chapter eleven, but here I want to make a different point: we can find common ground even when dealing with a slogan as condescending as this one.

By arguing that religious belief is against right reason, this atheist shows that he values rationality. To find some common ground, you can compliment him for that implicit commitment. You might say, "I heard you say religious belief is irrational. I think it's great that you value reason. In fact, if I thought my beliefs were irrational, I'd have trouble with them also. So I agree with you that we shouldn't hold things that are opposed to reason. Maybe you could explain more of what you have in mind?"

That may lead to a more cordial conversation about the issues. So even though it's not always easy, finding common ground is critical.

Tip 3: Explain an updated version of Pascal's Wager.

The seventeenth-century mathematician and Christian philosopher Blaise Pascal famously defended the idea that we should take into account practical considerations when it comes to believing in God or not. A simple version of the wager runs like this:

If you believe in God, and you're right, then you win the infinite good of eternal life with God. If you believe in God, and you're wrong, then you lose out on some temporary sinful pleasure in this life, but not much else. If you don't believe in God, and you're wrong, you risk the horrible outcome of eternal separation from God. If you don't believe in God, and you're right, you gain some temporary sinful pleasures in this life, but not much else.

So, given the stakes, the wise bet is to believe in God, even if you find the evidence for his existence to be mixed. Michael Rota, a Catholic philosopher, has defended an updated version of the wager that states that if you're about 50 percent confident that Christianity is true, then you should commit to living a devout Christian life.[109]

Now, atheists frequently criticize Pascal's Wager, but their criticisms can all be answered. Three popular objections to the wager are as follows:

- Objection 1: The wager encourages intellectual dishonesty; you can't force yourself to believe something that you don't actually believe.

- Objection 2: The wager doesn't tell you which God to believe in, and if you believe in the wrong God, then according to most religions, you're not any better off.

- Objection 3: The wager is un-Christian, since it makes Christianity out to be a self-centered endeavor by which we only believe in God for personal gain.

I contend that each of those objections can be answered effectively. Consequently, the wager stands as an important piece of the apologetics puzzle when presenting arguments for God. So let's look at how we might answer each objection.

Regarding objection number one, Rota's version of the wager completely sidesteps the issue of potential intellectual dishonesty in forcing oneself to believe. How so? Importantly, he describes the wager in terms of *religious commitment* rather than *belief.* In other words, he says a person should adopt a policy of committing to God and living a religious life even if he maintains interior reservations about the truth or falsity of God's existence. Adopting such a way of live naturally includes praying, aiming toward a life of virtue, and attending religious services. A person can pursue such a commitment even while not fully believing.

Prayers can be conditional. For example, an unconvinced person who commits to a religious life might pray, "God, if you exist, help me with X. Forgive me for Y" and so forth. And even while still in a state of agnosticism he can attempt to remove vices from his life. Finally, going to Mass or another religious event or service does not require someone to check his skepticism at the door. He can attend the service, pray, and participate in all of the parts where he feels comfortable.

In all these ways, a person can *commit* to living a devout Christian life, which sidesteps the issue of self-deception and forced belief.

Next, consider the second big objection to Pascal's Wager: that it says nothing about *which God* to pursue. Since there are "many gods" to choose from, the wager fails to present the choices accurately. It's not simply a choice between committing to God or not. It's a choice between committing to god number one, number two, etc., or none of the above. After all, most religions do not look kindly on those who believe in the wrong God, so Pascal's Wager does not present a helpful reason to seek any God in particular. This has come to be known as the "many gods" objection to Pascal's Wager.

How can we respond to this? Rota points out that the wager does not address the many options someone might have. But he also contends that there's a straightforward way to cut through this issue. Namely, commit to the God or religion that you think is most likely to be true.[110] In reality, there are not as many options as some skeptics make it seem. There are not 2,000 viable gods to choose from, as many often cited are widely acknowledged to be fictitious constructions, such as Zeus and Thor.

After examining the evidence and speaking with religious believers, a person can limit the options to a select few. Suppose a person finds himself 40 percent confident in Christianity, 15 percent confident in Islam, and 10 percent confident in Judaism. Then he can commit to that worldview he finds most likely to be true. Of course, assigning confidence levels to worldviews is hardly an exact science. Nonetheless, after viewing the philosophical, historical, and theological evidence for various positions, he can develop a disposition toward a particular one. And because theism provides such a high value if it is true, it's worth committing to that position.[111]

Finally, consider the third big objection to using Pascal's Wager: it makes Christianity a self-centered enterprise that endorses gambling to get the largest possible profit. This objection fails to consider what Christian commitment actually entails. For if someone commits to a devout Christian life, even if motivated out of an initially selfish concern, what sort of things will he do? Pray, aim to act virtuously, treat both neighbors and enemies with love, and so on.

Such actions are hardly consistent with a selfish lifestyle; on the contrary, they tend to foster a life of selflessness. Moreover, if Christianity is true, our ultimate happiness is to be found in God, and by living a Christian life we are more likely to help others grow close to God. Since the benefits are not just for ourselves, proceeding according to the wager does not have to be selfish.

Having answered those three big objections, we are ready to use Pascal's Wager in conversation. The value of Rota's version of the wager can hardly be overstated; it dramatically lowers the bar for natural theology. Perhaps one shudders in fear at the thought of presenting airtight, 100-percent-certain proofs of God's existence. According to Rota's version of the wager, we don't have to.

To show the power of potential consequences in deciding how to act, we could use the following illustration. Say, **"Suppose you walked by a fenced-in yard with a pool and what looked like a child lying face down in the pool. You weren't totally sure if it was a child or not—maybe you were 50 percent sure. What would you do?"**

Hopefully, your interlocutor would explain that he would act to find out if it was indeed a child and attempt to save him if possible. To enhance the illustration, you might add more details, **"Suppose you needed to break part of the fence, potentially getting scrapes or splinters, or damage some property in order to be able to see the pool or child. What should you do then?"**

This makes the decision a little more difficult, but he'll probably agree that minor injuries or property damage pale in comparison with the great good of saving a drowning child. Because of how valuable human life is, the right thing to do is to find out if there is a child drowning or not.

Similarly, if we find that there is a chance that God exists, even only a 50 or 40 or 30 percent chance, that reality is valuable enough to seek the truth about—even if it involves some bumps and bruises.

Arguments good enough to raise the likelihood of God's existence to around 50 percent should lead a person to devout religious commitment. After such a commitment, that person may find further arguments or religious experiences that bolster a steadfast, firm belief. So that's the third tip: **explain an updated version of Pascal's Wager.**

Tip 4: Maintain a calm, confident disposition.

Drawing upon my experience as a math teacher, I can attest to the fact that students trust a confident answer more than one delivered with palpable hesitancy. One can also look to the famous example of the Kennedy-Nixon presidential debates to see this idea at work. Whereas radio listeners thought the debate result was about even or that Nixon won, the vast majority of those watching on television found Kennedy to be the clear winner.[112]

Because of the way Kennedy showed confidence, viewers trusted more in what he had to say. Of course, if we are spewing abject falsehoods, no amount of confidence can repair them. But, if we are presenting good reasons to believe in God (or discussing any matter of the Faith), speaking calmly and confidently gives the evidence a better chance to land. Also, you should practice good speaking habits such as looking at the other person, offering nonverbal cues (such as nodding) to show them you are listening, and acknowledging common ground where possible.

As Catholics, we can increase our confidence in the Faith by entering an ever-deepening relationship with God. This can happen through daily prayer. It can happen through grace received in the sacraments. Over time, as we develop in our walk with God, more graces can lead to greater confidence in the Faith.

St. Paul reminds us, "Be watchful, stand firm in the faith, act like men, be strong. Let all that you do be done in love" (1 Cor. 16:13). By maintaining a calm, confident disposition we can present evidence to others so that it has the ring of truth.

Tip 5: Don't force final answers on the spot.

Do you remember *Who Wants to Be a Millionaire*, hosted by Regis Philbin? Contestants aimed to answer multiple-choice trivia questions to earn more and more money. One wrong answer meant "game over" for the contestants. After a contestant gave his answer, Regis would ask, "Final answer?" and the contestant would have to say "Yes" to lock it in. Frequently, that exchange created tension. With thousands of dollars on the line, contestants felt pressure as they aimed to make a final decision.

I would avoid this attitude in conversations with unbelievers. When someone feels pressed to make a final decision on the spot, his guard will go up. He may fear that he's being tricked or pressured into believing something. He may not be ready to make the commitment you are proposing. By forcing a final answer on the spot, you are more likely to let unbelievers off the hook of seriously considering the Catholic Christian worldview.

Again, I present anecdotal evidence from my mathematics classroom. Sometimes, as I attempt to explain how to solve a particular math problem, students raise concerns. They say, "I'm confused" or "I don't get it." Naturally, my response is usually, "What specifically is confusing you?" or "What specifically don't you get?" The most common responses I've heard to that question in my career are, "All of it" or "The whole thing."

In response, I restart the explanation of the problem, tracing the steps more slowly and deliberately. Yet occasionally a student will still express confusion: "I still don't get it!" At that point, if I attempt to go over the explanation again in a large group setting and get the student's thoughts along the way, he typically feels self-conscious and is reluctant to agree that he understands anything. Further explanations, even really good ones, do not help. And attempting to coerce the student to agree that he understands is only counterproductive.

Now, what's the point of that anecdote? If people resist being forced into agreement for even something as insignificant as a math problem, how much more will they resist being forced to give final answers to religious questions?

So you want to present the truth—but with a proper disposition that affords our discussion partners space to think about the issues and the freedom to revisit them. Instead of forcing a final answer on the spot, say, "I realize this may be the first time you've heard something like this and need to think about it more. Why don't you do that and let me know what you think next time." Then, in your next conversation, you can find out where the person is and work from there. While waiting, you can do short-term research into areas of that person's concern.

This process of accompaniment can apply to presenting evidence for God as well as the Gospel in its fullness. In *Evangelii Gaudium*, Pope Francis writes:

The Church will have to initiate everyone—priests, religious and laity—into this "art of accompaniment" which teaches us to remove our sandals before the sacred ground of the other (cf. Exod. 3:5). The pace of this accompaniment must be steady and reassuring, reflecting our closeness and our compassionate gaze which also heals, liberates and encourages growth in the Christian life.

Although it sounds obvious, spiritual accompaniment must lead others ever closer to God, in whom we attain true freedom. Some people think they are free if they can avoid God; they fail to see that they remain existentially orphaned, helpless, homeless. They cease being pilgrims and become drifters, flitting around themselves and never getting anywhere. To accompany them would be counterproductive if it became a sort of therapy supporting their self-absorption and ceased to be a pilgrimage with Christ to the Father (169-170).

From these passages, we learn that "accompaniment" involves the following:

- A "steady" and "reassuring" pace
- An aim of leading others "ever closer to God"
- An avoidance of "therapy" that supports "self-absorption"

Some might label this approach wishy-washy and too timid. But just because we do not force final answers on the spot does not mean we cannot proclaim the truth boldly. All this tip entails is that *after* bold proclamations space should be given to our dialogue partner to consider things over time. So accompaniment, the steady process of leading others to find true freedom and happiness in God, need not be timid. All I recommend is that you **don't force final answers on the spot.**

Tip 6: Remember that the world does not rest on your shoulders.

God's grace can work through imperfect conversations. When having conversations with real people about tough topics, things are going to get messy. You cannot expect to have all the answers and know exactly what to say in every scenario. In fact, if you wait until you've studied every possible argument and counter-argument before evangelizing, you will never actually do it!

Instead of refusing to enter conversations out of fear of messing up, change your mindset to that of a disciple in training. A disciple in training is willing to make mistakes and *learn from them*. To the disciple in training, bad conversations are not utter failures; they are opportunities to learn. You might even create a journal to document your evangelistic efforts and apologetic encounters. By recording your mistakes and meditating on your blunders, you can handle those issues even better the next time they arise.

Also, God's grace is at work even in the most imperfect dialogues. Although you might deem a particular encounter a failure, God can use your words to plant seeds in the minds of others that might lead to future spiritual growth. In the Bible, God constantly uses imperfect men to carry out his perfect plans. St. Peter denied the Lord three times. David committed adultery and murdered to cover it up. Yet Jesus was able to use these imperfect men to spread his message.

This shows that there is no limit to how God might use even what we deem our most ineffective encounters. So do not beat yourself up about bad conversations. Use them as opportunities to improve, and recognize that God can work through you in your worst moments.

Tip 7: Practice and share your testimony.

In John 4, Jesus meets and speaks with the Samaritan woman at the well.[113] She tells him "all she has done" and comes to understand that he is a prophet. After their conversation, she goes to and tells the townspeople about Jesus. Many are moved to believe because of her testimony. We read:

> Many Samaritans from that city believed in him because of the woman's testimony, "He told me all that I ever did." So when the Samaritans came to him, they asked him to stay with them; and he stayed there two days. And many more believed because of his word. They said to the woman, "It is no longer because of your words that we believe, for we have heard for ourselves, and we know that this is indeed the Savior of the world" (John 4:39–42).

It's clear that the testimony of believers can be a powerful witness and lead others to faith. It's also notable from verse 42 ("for we have heard for ourselves") that *after* the people were converted by the woman's own testimony, they enjoyed their own religious experience as they came to believe in the "Savior of the world."

That means our testimony might lead not only to conversions, but also to others having their own deep experiences of the Lord—which will in turn lead to them sharing testimony that can lead to even more conversions, and so on. But this virtuous chain reaction *begins* when we are willing to share our testimony. So how do we do that?

First, we must *practice* our testimony. If you listen to William Lane Craig share his testimony in a debate or some other setting, you will notice he tells his story almost the exact same way every time.[114] Yet each time I hear it, I am drawn in by it and find it to be an effective witness. So do not think that practicing and preparing your testimony ahead of time will make it seem "canned" or uninteresting.

To the contrary, through careful practice and revision, you can make your testimony as effective as possible.

Second, try to include the following fundamentals in your testimony: 1) how you have experienced God, 2) how it has changed your life over time, and 3) how it relates to the *kerygma*. The *kerygma* is the basic Christian message that God became man and dwelt among us; offered himself up for us as a sacrifice for sins; was crucified, died, and was buried; and rose from the dead to show that not even the grave could hold him—all so that God's grace in the beatific vision is made available to all, that they might come to know him and enjoy him forever.

Of course, how exactly that *kerygma* fits into your own story will require getting into your personal details. And I must admit, as a Catholic, that sharing my own testimony is never something I learned growing up, and the sound of it makes me uncomfortable. Nevertheless, I have two great recommendations to help you on this front:

1. The *Every Knee Shall Bow* podcast hosted by Michael Gormley and Dave VanVickle. They devote multiple episodes to how to craft and share your testimony effectively. They also have great stories from their years spent evangelizing.

2. *The Activated Disciple* by Jeff Cavins. This book contains an explanation of the *kerygma* and tons more. You will find practical tips for preparing your testimony and engaging in evangelization in the twenty-first century.

Finally, I want to add that sharing your testimony can show the *value and goodness* of Christianity, which is often overlooked by skeptical dismissals. Through a relationship with Christ, we can gain the greatest possible treasure, and such happiness can begin in this life and continue in the next. These considerations complement the point we made about Pascal's Wager and can increase the desire for others to cultivate belief in God. So, that's the seventh tip: **practice and share your testimony.**

Reasons Why People Resist the Evidence for God

No matter how well you present the evidence for God, or how swiftly you can answer the skeptic's objections, you'll still find that many people *resist* the evidence. Human beings are complex, and it's important to recognize that a failure to persuade someone does not mean that the arguments and evidence presented were poor. A good argument should not be judged by the number of people it persuades, but rather by how it accords with objective standards of reason and evidence.

Do not lose heart when atheists and skeptics walk away unconvinced. Sometimes, evangelization is more like a marathon than a sprint, and God can use a series of small conversations to slowly move someone to the truth of his existence in particular or Catholicism in general.

Now, since you are reading this book, you are probably interested in dialoguing with atheists and skeptics. So it's important to be aware of several reasons why people might be resistant to following the evidence where it leads. In what follows, I provide six reasons why some people may resist the evidence for God, and give suggestions for how to overcome that resistance.

For each reason, I give one suggestion for breaking through some of the resistance. These may help, but there are no money-back guarantees! Above all, make sure to pray that your atheist discussion partners can find what they need to have an abiding relationship with God.

Reason 1: They find religious belief irrelevant.[115] Perhaps your dialogue partner is simply indifferent toward religion. He does not think it is relevant to his life. He may not have any friends who take religion seriously. Cultural pressures no longer work in favor of Christianity in the United States and Europe (and perhaps other places as well). So if someone never encounters religious peers, it has become easier to go through life without confronting deep questions of religion. On top of that, the age of screens and social media provides a wealth of distraction for those who are indifferent about matters of faith.

One suggestion for responding to such apathy about religion is to ask some questions about deep topics. At first, these will likely feel uncomfortable. But after that initial discomfort, the person may show more interest in opening up to a deeper conversation. Ask, "Hey, I'm just curious, if God really does exist, wouldn't you want to have a relationship with him?" Or even something like this: "Hey, I'm just curious, what do you think happens after you die?"

These questions may lead the person to question his apathy and reconsider fundamental questions about the meaning of life.

Reason 2: They view religious believers as judgmental, arrogant, hypocritical, or some other negative label, so they do not want to associate with religion. If the very sounds and smells of Christians turns someone off, he is not in a position to examine evidence fairly. Also, if we're honest, we can all think of religious folks (even ourselves!) who have not always acted well toward others. Of course, the fact that some Christians do not practice Christian ideals is no reason to dismiss Christianity. But it can be a substantial obstacle to people who do not want to be caught dead living and acting like those arrogant, judgmental Christians. Now, the skeptic might be completely off-base in his characterization of Christians, but that's not the point at the moment. If we want to reach him, we should acknowledge his concerns as far as possible.[116]

One suggestion for responding to a person with such an obstacle is to offer sympathy. And, especially if it was the behavior of Catholics that bothers him, you could apologize on behalf of the Catholic Church for any maltreatment he received. Additionally, you could remind him that Catholics aim to follow Christ, who humbly dined with tax collectors and prostitutes. As we want to be "conformed to the image of [Jesus]" (Rom. 8:29), Catholics should strive to live holy lives of virtue and cast aside arrogance and hypocrisy. If we want people facing this obstacle to reconsider the Faith, we should start by humbling ourselves, offering sympathy, and, if appropriate, apologizing.

Reason 3: They have unrealistic expectations about how the evidence for God is supposed to work, or they have a deficient epistemology that blocks the evidence.

Some people approach an argument for the existence of God with an all-or-nothing, unrealistic attitude. That is, unless the argument persuades them that there must be a God in two minutes or less, it must not be a good argument. But such arguments are typically unavailable in most, if not all, disciplines. Imagine if someone held scientific arguments to that standard—as if to say, unless you can completely convince me in a few minutes that evolution or general relativity are true, then the arguments for them must not be any good. Anyone's failure to meet this standard would show precisely nothing. Sound arguments might take time, reflection, and philosophical training before their full import can be grasped. But it does not follow from that that they are not good arguments.

For example, it took the Catholic philosopher Edward Feser several years of teaching and investigating theistic arguments before he finally came to see their force.[117] Since then, he has come to be known as one of the sharpest thinkers in the domain of natural theology in our time. One suggestion for combating this unrealistic expectation about arguments is to ask your discussion partner if he would apply that standard to evolution or general relativity.

Another way an atheist can resist the evidence is by discounting all evidence that is not scientific. This view, known as scientism, is addressed earlier in chapter three. The fatal flaw of scientism is that it cannot meet its own test: the position that science is the only way of knowing is not something known through the scientific method. Since scientism is self-defeating, it cannot be consistently deployed as a way of dismissing evidence for God. Instead, people should be open to *all* possible evidence for a particular view, not only scientific but also philosophical and historical.

One suggestion for breaking through this resistance is to ask, "Suppose there's no direct, scientific evidence for God, but there's good evidence for God that comes to us in other ways. Would you be open to examining that?" Of course, your dialogue partner can just say no and stick to his scientism. But since scientism is self-defeating, we would hope he'd be open to relinquishing such a position.

Reason 4: They have internal obstacles to religious belief rooted in past experiences. Some unbelievers struggle to look past having been harmed by the Church or believers. Perhaps they were victims of sexual abuse. Perhaps they lost a loved one and did not receive any consolation from the Church. Perhaps they prayed for something for two decades and it never came to fruition. Perhaps they went to a priest with difficult questions they had about the Faith only to receive unsatisfactory answers. Perhaps they were told, "Just shut up and stop asking so many questions."

Regardless of the particulars of the bad experience, we must understand that people can have internal obstacles that took root long ago. As a result, they struggle to see the goodness and beauty of Catholicism, and they may struggle to take evidence for God seriously. This situation usually cannot be remedied by a single, strong presentation of the rational warrants for God. Instead, it will involve time, healing, and God's grace to move people back into a position where they can be more open to belief in God.

One suggestion for handling such internal obstacles is to pray for two things: 1) that your discussion partner be healed of any old wounds, and 2) that the right person may come into his life to undo the mistreatment he may have suffered. God's grace can reach those who have been badly hurt, and your friendship and prayer may be just what that person needs to take the next step toward faith.

Reason 5: They have internal obstacles to religious belief due to attachments to sin or current life circumstances. In his letter to the Romans, St. Paul writes:

For the wrath of God is revealed from heaven against all ungodliness and wickedness of men who by their wickedness suppress the truth. For what can be known about God is plain to them, because God has shown it to them. Ever since the creation of the world his invisible nature, namely, his eternal power and deity, has been clearly perceived in the things that have been made. So they are without excuse; for although they knew God they did not honor him as God or give thanks to him, but they became futile in their thinking and their senseless minds were darkened (1:18-21).

Some argue that this analysis applies to *all* unbelievers. They are *all* guilty of "suppressing the truth" in unrighteousness. Others say that Paul is drawing attention to a general pattern among those who resist God's calling. In his commentary on Romans, Scott Hahn writes of these verses:

> It is a question not of ignorance but of people's willful efforts to smother the truth under a heap of sinful choices and distractions. Failure to acknowledge a personal God—one Supreme Being, Lawgiver, and Intelligence—is first and foremost a moral problem. Only secondarily can it be called an intellectual problem.[118]

However widely Paul intends this analysis to apply, we must recognize it as a truth of our faith that people can "suppress the truth" and become "darkened" by sinful choices. I do *not* recommend voicing this directly to someone in a first conversation. But you must recognize the reality that people sometimes resist religion because of sinful attachments or a fear that the price of religious commitment will be too high.

For example, consider people who know what the Church teaches on homosexuality, divorce and remarriage, and abortion. Then suppose they are currently living in a situation directly contrary to Catholic sexual ethics. Perhaps they are living with a same-sex partner and have even obtained a state-issued marriage license, despite what the Church teaches about marriage and same-sex unions.[119] Perhaps they have been divorced and remarried without an annulment. Perhaps they are actively seeking an abortion or advising a friend to have one.

In such cases, people who do not want to relinquish their lifestyles or choices may resist so much as considering evidence for Catholicism. They might come across as skeptics who just want more evidence, but in reality, no reasonable amount of evidence will be able to overturn the resistance.

Although sin affects people in different ways, it's a fact of life that all of us must deal with the temptation to sin. We must pray daily and seek God's grace to live as he truly wants us to. You will never really know a person's heart to the point that you can pinpoint how much of his resistance is based on sinful desires.

You won't be able to say, well in the case of Jim it's 60 percent his sinful desires, another 20 percent ignorance, and 20 percent bad experiences. Those kinds of calculi do not take into account the complexities of human psychology. Moreover, only God can judge the heart. Our job is to do our best to evangelize others while realizing that sinful tendencies may prevent them from seeing the evidence clearly. In the case of friends, it might one day lead to us confronting them about the way they are living; but such fraternal correction should be done only out of love and when there is a reasonable prospect of success.

One suggestion for helping people living in a circumstance contrary to Church teaching (or with some other attachment to sin) is to point them to others who were in their position yet were able to change their lives. For example, when it comes to same-sex attraction, two excellent documentaries show the stories of people who are attracted to people of the same sex yet now desire to live according to Church teaching on the manner. The documentaries are available for free online: *The Third Way* and *Desire of the Everlasting Hills*.

Reason 6: They have studied the issues more than the person presenting the evidence and have serious objections that have gone unanswered. This final reason can be found among academic philosophers who have become atheists.[120] Perhaps they faced difficult questions about religion in high school or college. Upon confronting parents, friends, and local Church leaders, they received no satisfactory answers. So they came to reject religious belief altogether. They later researched atheism more deeply and never came across satisfactory arguments for faith.

When dealing with resistance rooted in intellectual difficulties, you may not be prepared to answer an atheist's questions. If he has studied the issues for years and looked into some answers and found them wanting, you want to commend him for having done his homework.

One further suggestion is to point him to an advanced resource that deals with his concerns in some depth. For example, if a philosophy-minded individual has serious objections to God's existence based on divine hiddenness, you might point him to Michael C. Rea's book *The Hiddenness of God*. He addresses the problem at a high level, and it might help your discussion partner to know that such work is being done by those who believe in God.

SUMMING UP

In this appendix we examined seven tips for presenting evidence and six reasons why some people resist evidence. Though the tips are by no means "magic bullets," they should be kept in mind if you want to improve your conversations with skeptics. As you have more conversations, you might develop your own tips and reminders that can be added to that list.

Regarding the six reasons why some people resist evidence, you may not be able to judge which (if any) are holding back a particular atheist. But you can keep those in mind and use the suggestions, where appropriate, to help someone overcome his resistance to God.

Nonetheless, after twenty chapters answering slogans and another chapter on tips for presenting evidence, you might be wondering: Okay, DeRosa, so what actual evidence do you suggest we use in conversation? Why should we think God actually exists? It is to that subject we turn next.

- Seven tips for presenting the evidence for God:
  - Tip 1: Stick to the *listen-reason-propose* framework.
  - Tip 2: Find common ground and voice this.
  - Tip 3: Explain an updated version of Pascal's Wager.
  - Tip 4: Maintain a calm, confident, and interested disposition.
  - Tip 5: Don't force final answers on the spot.
  - Tip 6: Practice and share your testimony.
  - Tip 7: Remember that the world does not rest on your shoulders.
- Six reasons why some people may resist the evidence for God:
  - Reason 1: They find religious belief irrelevant.
  - Reason 2: They view religious believers as judgmental, arrogant, or hypocritical and do not want to associate with them.
  - Reason 3: They have unrealistic expectations about how the evidence for God is supposed to work, or they

have a deficient epistemology that blocks the evidence.

- Reason 4: They have internal obstacles to religious belief rooted in past experiences.

- Reason 5: They have internal obstacles to religious belief due to current circumstances or attachments to sin.

- Reason 6: They have studied the issues more than the person presenting the evidence and have serious objections that have gone unanswered.

Five Arguments for God's Existence

Why should we believe in God? Even as you answer the slogans we looked at (and others), inevitably the conversation will steer back to the evidence for God's existence. Maybe a skeptic will acknowledge that his glib one-liners didn't have the force he once thought, but in the absence of any *actual reasons* to think God is real, he's content to go on living as an atheist.

There are many good theistic apologetics books worth reading, and my summary here of five arguments isn't a replacement for them. But it's a good outline and starting point for when your conversation partner wants to hear positive evidence.

GOOD REASONS TO BELIEVE IN GOD

Not all of these arguments have the same force or weight. And they are by no means the only arguments we could make. But over the years I have found these to be good arguments with distinctive features that make them useful in conversation. Note that I preface all the arguments with the indefinite article (as opposed to saying, for example, "*The* Kalam cosmological argument") because different versions of these arguments have been defended by different authors in different ways.

1. A Kalam Cosmological Argument
2. A Contingency Argument
3. An Argument from Reason
4. A Fine-tuning Argument
5. A Moral Argument

A KALAM COSMOLOGICAL ARGUMENT

Developed by Muslim philosophers in the middle ages, this argument for God's existence was famously reintroduced into Christian apologetics by William Lane Craig.[121] The core syllogism of the argument, which we have mentioned elsewhere, is simple and well-known:

Premise 1: Everything that begins to exist has a cause.

Premise 2: The universe began to exist.

Conclusion: Therefore, the universe has a cause.

Having reached the conclusion that the universe must have a cause, we can do a conceptual analysis of the cause and derive various attributes (timelessness, immateriality, and so forth) and finally argue the best explanation of the conclusion that the universe has a cause with these attributes is that God exists. That's a quick overview of the path one can take in defending a Kalam cosmological argument.

In chapter five, I gave reasons for the core syllogism so I will not rehearse those here. Yet, a common question we'll hear after arguing for the conclusion is, "Ok, but why should we think that the cause of the universe is God?" Let's look at some more details for why God is the best explanation of the beginning of the universe.

Note that the cause of the universe must exist independently of the universe. If the universe *came into being,* then its cause cannot be part of the universe itself. Since the universe contains all space, time, matter, and energy, the cause must therefore transcend those categories. This seems to follow from a secure principle: if something exists independently of X, then it cannot depend on X for any of its essential attributes.

So, we can say the cause is *immaterial,* since it precedes and exists independently of matter. Also, the cause is *spaceless* and *timeless,* since it precedes and exists independently of time and space. Moreover, since the cause goes beyond the universe, we can rightly call it *transcendent.*

Next, consider that *power* is the ability to make something happen. It follows that the cause of the universe has the *power* to cause the universe, otherwise the universe would never have begun to exist. The cause must also possess such power *eternally,* since it exists apart from the creation of the finite timeline.

At this point, we have conceived of a transcendent, immaterial, spaceless, timeless, eternally powerful cause of the universe.

Must we conclude that this transcendent cause is also a *person,* though? Someone might object that it might still be some undiscovered impersonal *force* or phenomenon. Craig has offered several reasons to think the cause of the universe is personal as opposed to impersonal. Let's look at two of them.

Reason 1: A Mind is the Only Viable Candidate

If we examine the candidates for what a transcendent, immaterial cause might be, not many come to mind. What would a reality that has no matter or spatial dimension be like? We can only imagine two candidates: 1) abstract objects and 2) minds.

Abstract objects (for example, the number seven), if they exist, would be not be material entities. However, they have no causal powers so they could not possibly be the transcendent cause of the universe.

On the other hand, being acquainted with our own minds we know that they have causal abilities. So an unembodied mind-like reality would fit the bill for being an immaterial, transcendent cause. While this argument does not yield metaphysical certainty, it serves as a plausible reason to think the cause of the universe is personal.

Reason 2: Forces Can't Choose

We have established that the universe began to exist. But *why* did it begin to exist? If all of the necessary antecedent conditions to create the universe were always in place in an impersonal way, it seems that the universe would have to be eternal. But we have established that the universe is not eternal.

In order for the universe to have been created a finite time ago, it seems that the cause must have something analogous to a *will* or *choosing power*. In other words, the universe could only begin to exist by virtue of the *creative initiative* of the cause. But impersonal forces do not possess a will or exercise creative initiative, so an impersonal force cannot explain why the universe came to be.

To summarize what we have said, through conceptual analysis and philosophical argument, we arrive at a *spaceless, timeless, immaterial, transcendent, eternally powerful cause of the universe that is plausibly personal*. What best explains this? Might there be two causes of such a type? Or fifty-seven? Scientists often employ a principle that causes should not be multiplied beyond necessity. So, the best explanation for such a cause is that God exists.

A CONTINGENCY ARGUMENT

This argument is a *metaphysical demonstration* that depends on some core definitions and principles. First, we must know what we mean by *being, contingent being,* and *necessary being*.

By *being*, we mean anything that has reality. A proton, a squirrel, and a dream you had last week all count as beings. Whether living or non-living, mental or extramental, anything at all that somehow has existence falls under the umbrella term *being*.

By *contingent being*, we mean something that exists but doesn't *have* to exist. For example, I, John DeRosa, am an example of a contingent being. I exist, but I do not *have to* exist. If my parents never met, I would not be here as I am. Most dialogue partners will readily grant that at least one contingent being exists, which is all we need to get the argument going. But before we proceed, we need to clarify the last piece of terminology.

A *necessary being* is anything that is not a contingent being. In other words, it is something that *must exist* and couldn't possibly not exist. At this point of the argument, we do not claim to know that such a being actually exists; we simply put forth a definition.

To recap our terms:

- Being = anything that exists
- Contingent being = something that exists but doesn't have to exist
- Necessary being = something that *must* exist and couldn't possibly not exist

Next, we need an important principle related to contingent beings. Since any contingent being exists but doesn't have to exist, we see that it *points outside of itself* to a cause for its existence. I am a contingent being, and I can point to my parents as causes of my existence. Obviously, I did not cause myself to exist, since I cannot be prior to myself.

The next part of the argument consists of a thought experiment. Suppose that all of reality consisted of one contingent being. It could be a quark, an atom, or a duck. Whatever you choose, suppose one contingent being were all there is. Of that scenario we can ask: *is it possible to have a world like that?*

Recall that a contingent being must point outside of itself to a cause for its existence. But if there were only one contingent being, there is nothing to point to as its cause.

We can rule out a few other suggestions. *Nothing* (nonbeing) cannot be the cause of this contingent being, since *nothing* is just the absence of being, and it has no causal powers and no abilities since it is not anything at all.[122] The contingent being cannot have *caused itself*, since, as have seen, in order to do so it would need to have existed *prior to* existing, which is impossible. So we have shown that the scenario with only one contingent being is incoherent.

But what if we add a second contingent being? Suppose we have a world with just two contingent beings: X and Y. Is that possible? Again, we run into an incoherent situation.

If X is a contingent being, then it must point outside of itself to a cause of its existence. The only candidate for such a cause is Y. So, Y can be the cause of X coming into being. But, if Y is also contingent, what caused Y to come into being? Nothing else remains in our world (X can't be the cause of Y for the same reason it can't be the cause of itself—it would need to have existed prior to Y, its cause). So, Y must have a cause and yet there is nothing that could be its cause. We have reached a contradiction.

What about a world with three contingent beings? Perhaps you can see where this is going. Positing a world with merely three contingent beings, or five, or ten, or billions, runs into the same problems of incoherence. If a world *only* has contingent beings, we will be left with an incoherent scenario. Therefore, we conclude, it is not the case that our world contains only contingent beings.

It follows from this analysis that there must be *at least one* necessary being: a being that *must* exist and couldn't possibly not exist.[123] A being in which there is no distinction between *what* it is (essence) and *that* it is (existence). With some further arguments[124] we could show this being must be the absolutely unique, intelligent, and the loving creator of all that exists. And so we have a second reason to think God exists.

AN ARGUMENT FROM REASON

Famously defended by C.S. Lewis in chapter three of his book *Miracles*, this argument aims to show that we ought to reject naturalism as inconsistent with reason.

In the naturalistic view, the entire world is exhausted by physical forces, laws of nature, and molecules in motion. Sure, these molecules can coalesce in ways that leads to the emergence of a wide variety of living and non-living realities, but physical stuff is all there is and all there ever will be.

On those assumptions, we run into a problem when analyzing our own thoughts, cognition, and rationality. For atoms, molecules, and particles do not have the property of *being true* or *being false*. They simply *are*. For example, we would never say this H_2O molecule is true but some other H_2O molecule is false.

What can we then say about our own rationality, which is chock-full of thoughts, cognitive processes, and beliefs? Can we say that some thoughts are true while others are false? According to naturalism, those thoughts can simply be reduced to the various firing of neurons and chemical reactions. Does it make sense to call one neural firing *true* and a different one *false*? If, as according to naturalism, neural firings are subject to the same analysis as water molecules, the answer must be no. Where does that leave us?

Lewis points out that it leads to a self-defeating skepticism, reducing all our rational endeavors to non-rational forces that are neither true nor false. If that is the case for all our beliefs, then it applies to anyone who forms the belief that naturalism is true. In other words, anyone who believes that naturalism is true can have no reason to suppose that any of his beliefs are true or false (since they are merely the byproducts of non-rational factors). Thus, affirming the statement "Naturalism is true" is self-defeating.

In light of this, the argument continues, we ought to reject naturalism and embrace a worldview that transcends the physical reduction of objects to atomic and sub-atomic bits. If naturalism is false, then some form of *super*naturalism must be true. This raises the probability and credibility of theistic worldviews. The existence of an intelligent Creator provides a perfect reason to expect that we would find creatures that have a reasoning ability capable of transcending natural categories. So, I submit, the argument from reason provides good evidence to support the view that God exists.

A FINE-TUNING ARGUMENT

Some people incorrectly assume that evidence for evolution has overthrown evidence for design. Although some forms of design may not point to a creator in light of evidence for biological evolution, the *fine-tuning* evidence still very much points to an intelligent Creator of the universe. Since about the mid-twentieth century, physicists have become more and more acquainted with "finely tuned" constants and quantities that fall in an extraordinarily narrow range such that if they were altered by the slightest amount, no life could ever form anywhere in the universe.[125]

While the details of a fine-tuning case can get technical, the general thrust of the argument should be intuitive:

Premise 1: The fine tuning of our universe for life is due either to *chance, necessity,* or *design.*

Premise 2: The fine tuning is not due to *chance* or *necessity.*

Conclusion: Therefore, the fine tuning is due to *design.*

The real force of the argument occurs in justifying premise 2. Why rule out necessity or chance?

Necessity suggests that the reason why the constants and quantities are finely tuned for life to arise is that they *had to be* that way. Some physical mechanism simply could not help but produce such a universe with those specific constants and quantities.

On the face of it, such a suggestion strikes me as implausible. Consider an analogy. Suppose you walked into a house and found an oddly shaped chair with many finely tuned features not found in typical chairs. Would we suppose that the manufacturers *just had* to make chairs that way based on the way their machines at the factory worked? That seems like a weird suggestion, and the more finely tuned features there were, the weirder it would seem. It would make much more sense to suppose that the manufacturer made chairs with those features for a specific purpose: for someone with diabetes, one arm, a stiff neck, arthritis in their left wrist, and so on.

Likewise weird is the idea that all the fine tuning in the universe is due to some necessity; unsurprisingly, physicists generally do not accept this explanation. This leads us to *chance* and to the *multiverse* theory—the most common objection to the fine-tuning argument.

According to this objection, there could be a universe generator of some sort that produces vast quantities of universes indefinitely. It may be unlikely for there to be just one universe with all these fine-tuned constants in the life-permitting range, but if you have *enough universes* being produced, eventually you are bound to get one that does the trick. So, perhaps we're just that lucky universe in a vast sea of other, non-life-permitting universes.

How might we respond? Some replies get very technical, but here's one suggestion. It seems that this universe generator is quite the specimen! If this physical mechanism has its own (immensely complex and finely tuned) intrinsic design and order, we need to ask: did the universe generator come about by *necessity*, *chance*, or *design*?

And so we see that positing a sophisticated universe generator does not eliminate the need for a designer—it just kicks the question back a step.

Since the multiverse itself seems to require fine tuning, the *chance* hypothesis fails as an ultimate explanation. So, we are left with *design*. The best explanation for the fine tuning of our universe is that God (a designing mind) exists. This argument can be added to our cumulative case to further raise the likelihood of theism.

A MORAL ARGUMENT

Ethics, the branch of philosophy devoted to studying morality, has given rise to a variety of arguments for God's existence. Over the centuries, different philosophers have proposed moral arguments that lead to the existence of a perfectly good foundation of reality, which we call God. The arguments vary in their overall approach and details; here are two examples.

First, we can argue that there are *objective moral facts* that must be grounded in a moral lawgiver. *Objective*, in this context, means that something is true independent of human opinion. Most reasonable people will agree that it seems just as wrong for someone to think that torturing children for fun is morally permissible as it is for someone to say two plus two equals five.

What accounts for this *objectivity* of moral facts? One answer is that there is a transcendent moral lawgiver who grounds them. Otherwise, morality would reduce to subjective preference, which flies in the face of our moral intuitions.

A common reply is that evolution programmed us to have strong moral intuitions for reasons related to survival. One problem with that proposal is it fails to ground the moral facts *as* facts. An evolutionary story for why creatures *think* something is objectively morally wrong does not sufficiently ground why it *is* morally wrong. On this view, moral facts do not come out to be facts at all but merely a byproduct of an innate delusion regarding their objectivity.

A second problem with the proposal is that it seems to lead to a repugnant consequence. For what if evolutionary survival pressures led human beings to think something like rape (which can propagate the species) was morally permissible? Would it still be objectively wrong? Those worldviews that provide an ultimate grounding for morality in a transcendent lawgiver can answer yes. Rape would still be objectively wrong, even if we had evolutionary instincts that it was permissible. However, it's unclear how atheists could affirm the same objectivity.

The best explanation of the objectivity of moral facts points us to a transcendent lawgiver.[126] That provides additional support for the thesis that God exists.

YOUR CUMULATIVE CASE

The *Catechism of the Catholic Church* speaks of a kind of sumtotal force when a variety of arguments are brought to bear in support of God's existence:

> Created in God's image and called to know and love him, the person who seeks God discovers certain ways of coming to know him. These are called proofs for the existence of God, not in the sense of proofs in the natural sciences, but rather in the sense of "converging and convincing arguments" . . . These "ways" of approaching God from creation have a twofold point of departure: the physical world and the human person (31).

If you want to enter discussions with atheists, you should commit to studying and developing your own list of "converging and convincing" arguments, over time adding details, principles, illustrations, and other techniques that can lead to more fruitful presentations. This appendix provides a description of five arguments that I like. As for whether they belong in *your* cumulative case—you can answer that only by investigating them, comparing them to other evidence, and deploying them in conversation.

ABOUT THE AUTHOR

John DeRosa is a high school teacher and the host of the *Classical Theism Podcast*. He lives in New Jersey with his wife, Christine.

ENDNOTES

1 *Every Knee Shall Bow* podcast, http://media.ascensionpress.com/category/ascension-podcasts/every-knee-shall-bow/.

2 Thomas V. Morris, ed., *God and the Philosophers: The Reconciliation of Faith and Reason* (New York: Oxford University Press, 1994), 62.

3 Greg Koukl, *Tactics: A Game Plan for Discussing Your Christian Convictions: Updated and Expanded (Grand Rapids, MI: Zondervan, 2019)*.

4 *Classical Theism* podcast, episode #51, "How to Discuss Worldview Issues with Others," http://www.classicaltheism.com/reason/.

5 For an outstanding treatment of how to speak truth in love, see the essay by Bryan Cross, "Speaking Truth in the Beauty of Love: A Guide to Better Online Discussion," available here: https://strangenotions.com/speaking-the-truth-in-the-beauty-of-love/.

6 J.P. Moreland, *Scientism and Secularism: Learning to Respond to a Dangerous Ideology (Wheaton, IL: Crossway, 2018), 31-32*.

7 Available at the Vatican website, http://www.educatio.va/content/dam/cec/Documenti/19_0997_INGLESE.pdf, 5.

8 That we have lost and need to recover the art of making arguments has been detailed by Bishop Robert Barron in his book *Arguing Religion (Des Plaines, IL: Word on Fire, 2018)*.

9 Catholics have a great deal of liberty to judge various components of evolutionary theories for themselves. For a Catholic approach to evolution, check out Fr. Nicanor Austriaco's website: thomisticevolution.org. For a Catholic who promotes Intelligent Design theory, check out Michael Behe's *Darwin Devolves*. For a dialogue on related issues between two Catholic scientists, Michael Behe and Stacy Trasancos, see this episode of the Pat Flynn Show: http://patflynnshow.libsyn.com/website/sunday-school-two-catholic-scientists-debate-intelligent-design.

10 Also, I'd love to hear them and share them on my podcast. Please send them to: jderosa@classicaltheism.com.

11 Edward Feser makes the case here for how apologetics works as an academic discipline: http://edwardfeser.blogspot.com/2014/05/pre-christian-apologetics.html.

12 See this podcast episode where Flynn makes that point: http://www.classicaltheism.com/flynn/.

13 Greg Koukl introduces the helpful analogy of gardening vs. harvesting. Often, when we have conversations with people about the Faith, we are part of the gardening process. Down the line, this gardening might lead to a grand harvest. The gardener played an integral role in the harvest by tiling the soil and watering seeds at the early stages. Similarly, apologetic encounters provide an opportunity to plant seeds that one day can be harvested. Find more details on Koukl's specific approach in Tactics.

14 At the time of this writing, the video has been restricted and is not publicly accessible. Nonetheless, you can see clips of Mehta's claims in *Capturing Christian-*

ity's response video here: https://www.youtube.com/watch?v=0XES1c60AXM.

15 Horn explains this updated version of the question in a recent dialogue on *The Counsel of Trent* podcast with Anthony Magnabosco: http://www.trenthorn. com/podcast/, episode #246.

16 Edward A. Feser, *Scholastic Metaphysics: A Contemporary Introduction, (Heusen-stamm, Germany: Editiones Scholasticae, 2014), 22.*

17 You can watch the exchange here: https://www.youtube.com/ watch?v=P5ZOwNK6n9U&t=177s.

18 Richard Dawkins, *Outgrowing God (New York: Random House, 2019), 5-6.*

19 You can watch the clip here for that argument: https://www.youtube.com/ watch?v=ZRLcJKUDZk8.

20 Pat Flynn's article: https://www.wordonfire.org/resources/blog/why-i-believe-in-one-more-god-than-the-atheists/24628/.

21 In fact, they are not similar to the God of classical theism. I explain that view of God in a PDF available here: www.classicaltheism.com/talkingpoints.

22 Herbert McCabe. *God Matters (New York, New York: Continuum International Publishing Group, 1987) 6-7.*

23 Example from https://randalrauser.com/2017/01/youre-atheist-respect-every-god-just-go-one-god-brief-reply/

24 This is a question Trent Horn recommends in the short video posted in the resources at the end of this chapter.

25 Craig Keener surveys and assesses various miracles in his two-volume work *Miracles: The Credibility of the New Testament Accounts* (Grand Rapids, MI: Baker Academic, 2011).

26 Many people, Christians included, have a view of the soul more like that of Plato or Descartes, whereas Catholics tend to follow Aristotle and Aquinas. For a better understanding of the different views of souls and minds, I recommend *Philosophy of Mind (Beginner's Guide)* by Edward Feser. The position more at home in Catholic thought is known as *hylomorphic dualism*, while Descartes' view is known as *substance dualism*. Faithful Catholics can hold either view, and there are a variety of subcategories and distinctions within those views.

27 For more on different views of the soul, including a defense of the Catholic view of hylomorphism, see Edward Feser's *Philosophy of Mind: A Beginners Guide* (London: Oneworld Publications, 2006).

28 Professor James Madden uses this example in multiple talks on neuroscience and the soul given through the Thomistic Institute. You can find all his talks and more at thomisticinstitute.org.

29 In part 3, I defend an argument for God's existences rooted in this transcendence. The editor of this also suggests *The Mind and the Brain* by Jeffrey Schwartz.

30 See his 2013 article at Catholic.com: https://www.catholic.com/magazine/ online-edition/does-it-matter-that-many-scientists-are-atheists?gclid=CjwKCA iA9JbwBRAAEiwAnWa4Q8BwHtO-sfKoaG68ZTOj8M0lpZalwHQWzI7_Xt_ JdoqohAvgtRs5mxoC7lMQAvD_BwE.

31 The study can be found here: https://www.pewforum.org/2009/11/05/scientists-and-belief/.

32 Their official website contains detailed information about their mission and

conferences: www.catholicscientists.org.

33 Find this information at the following page of their website: https://www. catholicscientists.org/join.

34 Elaine Ecklund's recent book *Science vs. Religion: What Scientists Really Think* shows that scientists are more religious than we realize. In the course of her interviews she found that many scientists reject religion for personal reasons prior to becoming scientists (as opposed to rejecting religion solely on scientific grounds).

35 Pope John Paul, *Fides et Ratio*, 1998.

36 The discussion was aired as an episode of the *Counsel of Trent* podcast. Link to the episode and transcript: https://www.catholic.com/audio/cot/is-it-rational-to-believe-in-miracles-part-1-with-john-loftus.

37 Interestingly enough, Edward Feser's conversion story reflects the fundamental points under discussion. He explains how he found David Hume's objections to miracles to be correct until he came to see that God exists. Then, he viewed the typical objections to the Resurrection in a much different light. Ultimately, he became a Catholic. The details of his story can be found in *Faith and Reason: Philosophers Explain Their Turn to Catholicism*, ed. Brian Besong and Jonathan Fuqua (San Francisco: Ignatius Press: 2019).

38 Tim McGrew provides some helpful criteria for narrowing down the specific miracle claims one should investigate. See his explanation on this episode of the Pat Flynn Show: https://patflynnshow.libsyn.com/the-philosophy-of-miracles-with-dr-tim-mcgrew.

39 The blog post can be found here: https://edwardfeser.blogspot.com/2017/09/flew-on-hume-on-miracles.html.

40 Gary Habermas, "My Pilgrimage from Atheism to Theism: An Exclusive Interview with Former British Atheist Professor Antony Flew." Available from the website of Biola University at www.biola.edu/antonyflew.

41 This book contains a sophisticated discussion of probability in its chapter on miracles. For more ammunition in debunking this slogan as well as David Hume's arguments against miracles, I recommend Craig's book.

42 Alexander Vilenken, "The Beginning of the Universe" online article, https://inference-review.com/article/the-beginning-of-the-universe.

43 Edward Feser, *Five Proofs for the Existence of God* (San Francisco: Ignatius Press, 2017).

44 Josh Rasmussen, *How Reason Can Lead to God* (Downers Grove, IL: IVP Academic, 2019). Rasmussen has a chapter-long defense of the concept of God having "eternal power."

45 See, for example, William Craig, *The Kalam Cosmological Argument* (New York: Barnes & Noble, 1979).

46 See, for example, J.L. Schellenberg, *Divine Hiddenness and Human Reason* (Ithaca, NY: Cornell University Press, 2006).

47 Michael Rea, *The Hiddenness of God* (New York: Oxford University Press, 2018). For another extended treatment of the argument, see Adam Green and Eleonore Stump, eds., *Hidden Divinity and Religious Belief: New Perspectives* (Cambridge, England: Cambridge University Press, 2015).

48 These premises are put forward in Ben Watkins's online article, "Why I Am an Atheist," https://capturingchristianity.com/ben-watkins-why-i-am-an-atheist/.

49 Rea, *The Hiddenness of God*, chapter 2, endnote 9.

50   As Jesus says in Matthew 7:7-8, "Ask, and it will be given to you; seek, and you will
      find; knock, and it will be opened to you. For everyone who asks receives, and he
      who seeks finds, and to him who knocks it will be opened."

51   Rea, *The Hiddenness of God*, 94.

52   Ibid., 129.

53   See CCC 390.

54   In CCC 43 we read, "Admittedly, in speaking about God like this, our language is
      using human modes of expression; nevertheless it really does attain to God himself,
      though unable to express him in his infinite simplicity. Likewise, we must recall that
      'between Creator and creature no similitude can be expressed without implying an
      even greater dissimilitude'; and that 'concerning God, we cannot grasp what he is,
      but only what he is not, and how other beings stand in relation to him.'" (The first
      quote is from Lateran Council IV and the second is from St. Thomas Aquinas, *Summa
      Contra Gentiles* I:30.)

55   "God: Supreme Being or Imaginary Friend?" available here: https://www.youtube.
      com/watch?v=_nC99sCxFbE. Also, Trent Horn debated Dan Barker a second time
      in 2018 on whether the Christian God exists. That debate can be found here: https://
      www.youtube.com/watch?v=bIuDfh-6iUs.

56   For a more in-depth analysis of this point see Rea, *The Hiddenness of God*, chapter 8.

57   Sometimes, the evidential problem is called the "probabilistic" problem of evil. Also,
      one may see it referred to as the problem of "gratuitous" evil or "mysterious" evil.
      What all of these problems have in common is that they use evil as evidence against
      God's existence without committing to the logical problem of evil.

58   Jimmy Akin surveys several possible responses to the question in an article at
      strangenotions.com entitled "Will We Have Free Will in Heaven?" You can read it
      here: https://strangenotions.com/will-we-have-free-will-in-heaven/. Also, Cameron
      Bertuzzi, who runs the website and YouTube channel *Capturing Christianity*, surveys
      several responses in a 2019 video. You can watch it here: https://www.youtube.com/
      watch?v=kOmOLre6CyM.

59   The *Catechism of the Catholic Church* allows that the Genesis story of the fall of Adam
      and Eve contains figurative language, yet it still refers to a real, historical event that
      took place at the dawn of human history (CCC 390).

60   Timothy Keller, *The Reason for God: Belief in an Age of Skepticism* (New York, New
      York: Penguin Group Inc., 2008), 23.

61   See this well-produced animated video by Reasonable Faith that provides an answer
      to the evidential problem of evil: https://www.youtube.com/watch?v=cxj8ag8Ntd4.

62   See this video for a presentation of the beauty and design of butterflies: https://www.
      youtube.com/watch?v=cxj8ag8Ntd4.

63   This point is argued by Joshua Rasmussen in *How Reason Can Lead to God*. By
      "mysterious evils" he means evils that are "so bad and so hard to explain that no human
      has any idea what reason a perfectly good being could have for allowing them" (160).

64   Rasmussen, *How Reason Can Lead to God*, 160.

65   Ibid.

66   Ibid., 161.

67   C.S. Lewis, *The Problem of Pain*, Chapter 6.

68   For an introduction to "classical theism" as opposed to theism more generally, see the free PDF "What Is Classical Theism and Why Should We Hold to It?" available here: www.classicaltheism.com/talkingpoints.

69   Brian Davies, *The Reality of God and the Problem of Evil* (New York, New York, Continuum International Publishing Group, 2006): 202-203.

70   Ibid., 204-205.

71   Ibid., 205-208.

72   Typically, the term "theodicy" refers to attempts to provide reasons to justify why God allows evil in the world.

73   Joshua M. Brown, *An Apophatic Response to the evidential argument from Evil* (International Journal of Philosophy and Theology, Volume 78, 2017).

74   Karlo Broussard, *Prepare the Way: Overcoming Obstacles to God, the Gospel, and the Church* (El Cajon, CA: Catholic Answers Press, 2018), 328-329.

75   Davies, *The Reality of God and the Problem of Evil,* Chapter 7.

76   Ben Watkins, "Why I Am an Atheist," https://capturingchristianity.com/ben-watkins-why-i-am-an-atheist/.

77   Feser, *Five Proofs of the Existence of God,* 302.

78   Richard Dawkins, *The God Delusion.*

79   See 1 Samuel 15:3 for instance.

80   Karlo Broussard, *Prepare the Way,* 243.

81   His statement can be found in this short YouTube clip of an interview of Tyson by Martha Teichner: https://www.youtube.com/watch?v=I0nXG02tpDw

82   *Summa Theologiae* II-II:2:9.

83   In part three of the book, where I present arguments for God's existence, I will also list resources for defending these aforementioned motives of credibility.

84   See chapter one for examples of "weak evidence."

85   Watch the full debate with Trent Horn on YouTube: https://www.youtube.com/watch?v=_nC99sCxFbE&t=2010s.

86   For example, some theists have attempted to reduce "lack-theism" to absurdity by saying it would imply rocks and infants are atheists, since they lack a belief in God. However, the obvious response from the atheist side is to clarify that atheists are those who lack a belief in God while being able to believe in him. So, on this clarified definition, rocks and infants would not be atheists, since they cannot form beliefs in God.

87   If one does want to take the path of challenging their definition of atheism, a good dialectical move would be to present well-known atheists who do not share the "lack-theism" definition. Professor Graham Oppy, one of the best-known living atheists, says this about the definition of atheism: "I have argued that we should characterize atheists and agnostics in terms of their doxastic attitudes towards the claim that there are no gods: atheists believe that there are no gods, agnostics suspend judgement whether there are no gods" (*Atheism and Agnosticism*, Cambridge, England: Cambridge University Press, 2018).

88   If it is close to fifty-fifty, Michael Rota argues that Pascal's Wager can kick in and provide a strong reason to commit to God. We examine this more in Appendix A.

89   In this episode of the *Pints with Aquinas* podcast, Matt Fradd and Edward Feser examine Dawkins's treatment of Aquinas's Five Ways and show that he does not successfully refute them: https://pintswithaquinas.libsyn.com/79-edward-feser-

explodes-richard-dawkins-refutation-of-aquinas-5-ways.

90 The blog post by Mano Singham can be found here: https://freethoughtblogs.com/
singham/2017/09/15/here-we-go-again-trying-to-prove-gods-existence/. Feser
took issue with Singham's attempt to "guess" the arguments in his book and offered a
reply here: https://edwardfeser.blogspot.com/2017/09/thought-free-blogs.html.

91 The video is titled "That's Offensive!" and at the time of this writing is available
here: https://www.youtube.com/watch?v=LofSg2HBaUE.

92 You can watch the full interview here: https://www.youtube.com/
watch?v=P5ZOwNK6n9U.

93 For a great introduction to the Bible, see *The Bible Is a Catholic Book* by Jimmy Akin
(El Cajon, CA: Catholic Answers Press, 2019).

94 The Catholic Church affirms that the Bible teaches without error as far as faith
and morals are concerned. Based on *Dei Verbum* 11, some have sought to reconstrue
Church teaching on inerrancy and restrict it *only* to faith and morals. However, the
more traditional understanding is that the biblical authors are protected from error in
all that they assert, on faith and morals or any other topic. However, it's not always
easy to figure out what precisely is being asserted. For a defense of the complete
doctrine of inerrancy over and against the restricted view, I recommend *Faith Comes
from What Is Heard: An Introduction to Fundamental Theology* by Lawrence Feingold
(Steubenville, OH: Emmaus Academic, 2016).

95 This article by the atheist Hemant Mehta includes that portion of the transcript:
https://friendlyatheist.patheos.com/2012/04/29/dan-savage-points-out-the-
hypocrisy-in-the-bible-so-young-journalists-walk-out-on-him/. As of this writing,
you can still find the clip on YouTube if you search "Dan Savage Bible Slavery."

96 Skeptics commonly cite Exodus 21:1-7 and Leviticus 25:44-46 as two difficult slavery
passages.

97 171, Bruce, F.F. *The International Bible Commentary* (Zondervan Publishing House: 1979).

98 This response can be viewed here on YouTube: https://www.youtube.com/
watch?v=6mmskXXetcg.

99 Plantinga, *Knowledge and Christian Belief*, 90.

100 I credit Jon McCray, creator of the YouTube channel *Whaddo You Meme*, for coming
up with this great question. You can watch his entire response to this objection here:
https://www.youtube.com/watch?v=oE1a-TuQ8J4.

101 It's important to affirm this point, i.e., that such people will still be saved *by Christ*
and *through his Church*, since the Catholic Church has taught definitively that there is
no salvation outside the Church. This is rooted in Jesus' teaching that he is "the way,
the truth, and the life" (John 14:6).

102 Thomists (typically Dominicans) usually deny that God has "middle knowledge."
Molinists (typically Jesuits) affirm it. A discussion of the related issues goes beyond
the scope of this book. For a defense of Molinism, see William Lane Craig's work
The Only Wise God: The Compatibility of Divine Foreknowledge and Human Freedom
(Eugene, OR: Wipf & Stock, 2000). For a critique of Molinism from a Thomistic
perspective, see *Predestination: The Meaning of Predestination in Scripture and the Church*
by Reginald Garrigou-Lagrange (Charlotte, NC: TAN Books, reprint ed., 1998).

103 See Feser, *Five Proofs of the Existence of God*, 249-260, for a detailed look at this slogan

and for documentation of both academic and popular atheists who have employed it.

104 Daniel Dennett, *Breaking the Spell: Religion as a Natural Phenomenon*, reprint ed. (New York: Penguin, 2007), 242. Quoted in Feser, *Five Proofs*, 252.

105 In chapter twenty-three, we defend Delfino's version of Aquinas's Third Way, which is a form of contingency argument.

106 Sam Harris, *The End of Faith: Religion, Terror, and the Future of Reason*, reprint ed. (New York: W.W. Norton, 2005), 27.

107 See this article for the full context of the quotation: https://zenit.org/articles/ cardinal-ratzinger-on-the-abridged-version-of-catechism/.

108 Charles Phillips and Alan Axelrod, *Encyclopedia of Wars*, 3 vols. (New York: Facts on File, 2004).

109 Michael Rota, *Taking Pascal's Wager: Faith, Evidence and the Abundant Life* (Downers Grove, IL: IVP Academic, 2016).

110 In an episode of the *Classical Theism* podcast, Rota spells out this thought in some more detail: www.classicaltheism.com/wager.

111 Some might wonder at what particular threshold Pascal's Wager kicks in. It's not necessary that we argue for a wager-like commitment for any slightest bit of likelihood. For example, some might wonder if holding a 0.01 percent chance that Christianity is true, and a lower confidence level for other religious worldviews, is enough to make it rational to commit to it. Rota does not defend such a scheme, as his version of the wager is geared toward those who have around a 50 percent confidence level in Christianity. What constitutes "around 50 percent?" Is 39 percent enough? Is 25 percent? These are interesting questions that go beyond the scope of this chapter. For a defense of the view that it can be rational to commit to Christianity with even a very small evidence-based confidence level, see Daniel McKaughn's article "Authentic Faith and Acknowledged Risk: Dissolving the Problem of Faith and Reason," *Religious Studies*, 49, no. 1 (March 2013): 101-124.

112 See this article for some more background and context of the Kennedy-Nixon debates: https://www.history.com/topics/us-presidents/kennedy-nixon-debates.

113 For a detailed exegesis of this chapter with application to salvation history, I recommend Brant Pitre's *Jesus the Bridegroom: The Greatest Love Story Ever Told* (New York: Image Books, 2018).

114 For one example, see the YouTube video "William Lane Craig's short testimony," available here: https://www.youtube.com/watch?v=KkAAE2_vLsY.

115 For a full-length treatment of the subject of religious indifference, check out Matt Nelson's book *Just Whatever: How to Help the Spiritually Indifferent Find Beliefs That Really Matter* (El Cajon, CA: Catholic Answers Press, 2018).

116 "As far as possible" does not mean you should lie and agree with him when he speaks falsely. Rather, aim to sympathize with his description.

117 You can find Feser's full conversion story in *Faith and Reason: Philosophers Explain Their Turn to Catholicism*, previously cited. It's a great read.

118 Scott W. Hahn, *Romans* (Grand Rapids, MI: Baker Academic, 2017), 13.

119 For the Church's teaching on homosexuality and same-sex attraction see CCC paragraphs 2357-2359. For Church teaching on the sacrament of marriage see CCC paragraphs 1601-1658. For an outstanding treatment of how Catholics can approach

these issues in a loving way, I recommend the book *Made for Love: Same-sex Attractions and the Catholic Church* by Fr. Mike Schmitz.

120 In an episode of the *Classical Theism* podcast, Tomas Bogardus, a Catholic, relays anecdotal evidence precisely along these lines: www.classicaltheism.com/burdenofproof.

121 William Lane Craig, *The Kalam Cosmological Argument* (Eugene, Oregon: Wipf and Stock Publishers: 1979).

122 The physicist Lawrence Krauss wrote a book called *A Universe from Nothing*, but many have pointed out how he equivocates on the term *nothing*. What the universe comes from in Krauss's analysis is not the same thing that metaphysicians mean by *nothing*. When I use *nothing* here, I refer to the philosophical sense of *nothing* such that it refers to a universal negation and a complete absence of being.

123 Aquinas distinguished between something being *necessary through itself* and *necessary through another*. A common illustration goes like this. Imagine a world where the sun existed eternally and necessarily. So, the sun's rays have eternally shined upon various planets and provided warmth. Now, are the sun's rays necessary? Yes, since they will be necessarily shining as the sun has existed necessarily and eternally. Yet, we would say the sun's rays are still *dependent* upon the sun. In other words, the rays would not be necessary unless the sun also existed necessarily. In this way, the rays are necessary *through another*, namely, the sun. Through that example, we can ascertain that beings necessary *through another* always point outside of themselves to a source of their necessity, and therefore there must still be a being that is necessary through itself.

124 For details on those additional arguments, see *Does God Exist?* By Matt Fradd and Robert A. Delfino, 62-68.

125 For details on the fine-tuning, see *A Fortunate Universe* by Luke Barnes.

126 There is tension with some moral arguments and traditional natural law theory. For this reason, I refrain from expressing *precisely how* the objective moral facts trace back to God. Some divine command theorists would ground such objectivity immediately in God's commands. However, Thomists who defend a natural law approach would ground the objectivity of moral facts in the *natures of things*, which flourish or fail to flourish as the kinds of things they are. Some might think this wipes out the argument for God we had in mind. I do not agree. Rather, we can ask how did things ultimately get their natures and make an argument along the lines of Aquinas's Fifth Way. It's true that such a move does not have the exact same flavor as the moral argument given by a divine command theorist, but it still leads to an intelligent creator. For a defense of the Fifth Way of St. Thomas Aquinas, I recommend *God is No Delusion: A refutation of Richard Dawkins* by Fr. Thomas Crean, O.P. (Ignatius Press: 2007). For more details on the "tension" I describe above, see the chapter on *Ethics* in *Aquinas: A Beginner's Guide* by Edward Feser (One World Publications: 2009).